86121 4303 1813 £6.25

C000296395

PERGAMON INTERNATIONAL
of Science, Technology, Engineering ar
The 1000-volume original paperback library i
industrial training and the enjoyment of leisui
Publisher: Robert Maxwell, M.C.

Messing About in Problems

An Informal Structured Approach to their Identification and Management

This book is the first volume in a new international book series

FRONTIERS OF OPERATIONAL RESEARCH
AND APPLIED SYSTEMS ANALYSIS

General Editor: Rolfe Tomlinson

The series is aimed at helping practitioners to broaden their subject base
and to advise managers and specialists in related areas of important new
developments in the field.
The scope of the books will be broad and their authorship international.
The subject is interpreted widely to include any scientific, applied, interdisciplinary and systems-oriented approach to the study of real-life decision
problems.
Rolfe Tomlinson is Professor of Systems and Operational Research at the
School of Industrial and Business Studies at the University of Warwick, and
is President of the European Association of OR Societies. He was for many
years the Director of Operational Research at the National Coal Board and
was then Area Chairman for Management and Technology at the International Institute of Applied Systems Analysis. The series will reflect his
deep belief that scientific systems-oriented research can be of direct
practical use over a much wider range of topics than at present, but only
if the work is problem-oriented and seen as a collaborative effort with the
problem owner.

Volume 2
TOMLINSON R. & KISS, T.
Rethinking the Process of Operational Research and Applied Systems
Analysis

Volume 3
KINGSMAN, B.
Raw Materials Purchasing: An Operational Research Approach

A Related Journal
JOURNAL OF THE OPERATIONAL RESEARCH SOCIETY*
Published on behalf of the Operational Research Society Limited, London

Editor: Professor K. B. Haley, Department of Engineering Production,
University of Birmingham, P.O. Box 363, Birmingham B15 2TT,
England

This journal publishes contributions on any matter relevant to the theory,
practice, history, or methodology of Operational Research or the affairs of
the Society. It is aimed at applications in any field and encourages the
submission of accounts of good, practical case studies illustrating OR in
action; of reviews of the state of development of fields of knowledge
relevant to OR; and of controversial articles on methodology, technique
or professional policy.

*Free specimen copy sent on request

Messing About in Problems

An Informal Structured Approach to their Identification and Management

by

COLIN EDEN

SUE JONES

and

DAVID SIMS

Centre for the Study of Organizational Change and Development
University of Bath, UK

PERGAMON PRESS

OXFORD · NEW YORK · TORONTO · SYDNEY · PARIS · FRANKFURT

U.K.	Pergamon Press Ltd., Headington Hill Hall, Oxford OX3 0BW, England
U.S.A.	Pergamon Press Inc., Maxwell House, Fairview Park, Elmsford, New York 10523, U.S.A.
CANADA	Pergamon Press Canada Ltd., Suite 104, 150 Consumers Rd., Willowdale, Ontario M2J 1P9, Canada
AUSTRALIA	Pergamon Press (Aust.) Pty. Ltd., P.O. Box 544, Potts Point, N.S.W. 2011, Australia
FRANCE	Pergamon Press SARL, 24 rue des Ecoles, 75240 Paris, Cedex 05, France
FEDERAL REPUBLIC OF GERMANY	Pergamon Press GmbH, Hammerweg 6, D-6242 Kronberg-Taunus, Federal Republic of Germany

First edition 1983

Library of Congress Cataloging in Publication Data
Eden, Colin.
Messing about in problems.
(Frontiers of operational research and applied systems analysis; v. 1) (Pergamon international library of science, technology, engineering, and social studies)
Includes bibliographical references.
1. Problem solving.   I. Jones, Sue.   II. Sims, David.
III. Title.   IV. Series.   V. Series: Pergamon international library of science, technology, engineering and social studies.
HD30.29.E3   1983   658.4'03   82-25967

British Library Cataloguing in Publication Data
Eden, Colin.
Messing about in problems.—(Frontiers of operational research and applied systems analysis; v. 1).—(Pergamon international library)
1. Operations research
I. Title   II. Jones, Sue   III. Sims, David,
1948—   IV. Series
001.4'24   T57.6

ISBN 0-08-029961-X (Hardcover)
ISBN 0-08-029960-1 (Flexicover)

Printed in Great Britain by A. Wheaton & Co. Ltd., Exeter

Preface

All OR practitioners, and indeed all professional investigators, learn early in their careers that the problems facing them are not neatly packaged, nor do solutions fall out as if they were puzzles in a daily newspaper. They find themselves in a 'mess' — to use Ackoff's phrase — in which uncertainty and conflict are the essence of the problem rather than a nuisance element to be eliminated before the real work begins. Colin Eden and his team at Bath University have pioneered research in this area for many years, based on direct consulting experience. This book brings together this experience in a comprehensive and readable form, which makes it useful reading for all, whether they are professional investigators or not, who have to attempt to unravel problems in an organizational context.

ROLFE TOMLINSON
General Editor

Contents

Introduction

This book is aimed at all those working in and around organizations who are interested in ways of thinking systematically and creatively about messy problems, whether their own or other people's, they are called upon to help with. It is about the ideas, approaches and methods we have developed over the past few years out of working with individuals and groups who see their problems as complicated, messy, not readily quantifiable, but who nevertheless would like some systematic analysis techniques to manage them. It is not intended to offer ideas which supplant those already found useful, quantitative or qualitative. Rather we are suggesting ways of thinking about problems, and techniques to handle them, which may be complementary to others by retaining the explicitness of many quantitative techniques alongside the sensitivity and flexibility of some qualitative techniques.

We want to introduce our ideas to the interested layman as well as to the social scientist, consultant, or psychologist. Nevertheless, the book is mostly aimed at those persons in organizations who believe it is their business to be a service to others by helping them think more explicitly and deliberately about the problems they face. In organizations we can identify large numbers of people who depend, for their own satisfaction and for their occupational well-being, upon being seen as 'helpful' to others. They are mostly people with a service or staff function. In most organizations they are found in departments such as marketing services, personnel services, training, corporate planning, organizational development, operational research, systems analysis, internal consultancy and management services. Each of these groups depends, in part, for their success upon their ability and skills at understanding the nature of the problems their clients own and finding a role within the context of their expertise and the problem as the client sees it.

There is, however, another group of persons who might find the ideas contained in this book helpful. Several writers, including Galbraith and Toffler, have discussed the way in which increasing specialization may lead to organizations being structured around semi-permanent project teams. It is common for leaders of such teams to face considerable difficulties in effectively managing the ideas and decisions within an interdisciplinary team. The methods we develop in this book have shown themselves to be particularly helpful to project team leaders.

AN OVERVIEW

It is traditional for authors to use the introductory chapter to provide an overview of the contents, and a guide to the options open to the reader. We shall do this, but more importantly we want to give warning of what each chapter is trying to get you to believe – what points of view we wish to indoctrinate into your thinking and your practical problem helping.

Chapter 1 describes a world of organizational life which will most probably be recognizable to you, and can act as a contextual setting for the remainder of the book. Most books on the nature of organizations choose to describe the formal and structural aspect of the organization as a system. We shall not write about organizations in this way because we do not believe that these aspects are the most relevant to understanding the nature of problems which in our experience belong to individuals or small groups. We shall argue that organizations are social entities where problems are to do not with objectivities and organizational goals but subjectivities and negotiated orientations. Problems and decision-making are predominantly set within politics, interpersonal considerations, idiosyncratic values, and personal perspectives. The view we present is not original – indeed it is common sense – but it is unusual as the context for a book on problem-solving. Our view is thus that notions of 'rationality' and 'objectivity' in organizational decision-making are unhelpful to developing ways of helping people with their problems.

At the end of Chapter 1 we begin a case study example which unfolds throughout the rest of the book as a practical illustration of the ideas set out in each chapter. This is intended to add a context for those ideas to help readers imagine how they might put them into effect in their own working environment.

The second chapter establishes the link between our view of organizations and the problems that belong to people and small groups. We shall try to demonstrate that problems are psychological entities which are often unclear and expressed as anxiety and concern about a situation as well as being expressed as a positive wish for the situation to be different in a particular way. Problems are idiosyncratic constructions that belong to individuals and not to the 'world out there'. We shall consider possible approaches to the relationship between a problem-helper and his client, and argue that a view of problems as personal constructions leads to adopting a negotiative, rather than coercive or empathetic paradigm for problem-helping. We also suggest that a process of assisting the defining and formulation of a problem is a crucial and often neglected precursor to any attempts to solve it. This means that the starting point for helping with problems is through devising a way of listening to the problem-owner which will mean that it is possible to see the world from his point of view. The art of listening is not at all easy and needs the development of particular skills.

The third chapter specifically considers ways of listening to a problem in such a way that a model or representation of the ideas, beliefs, images, and values can be fed back. We do not presume that all individuals either want to, or are able to, articulate the subjective view they have of a problem. We therefore introduce a range of techniques for helping the helper encourage the communication of the important aspects of the problem. The tendency for organizationally based problems to be expressed in the light of particular norms, or not to be expressed because of subjectivity, lack of evidence, or politics and interpersonal considerations is considered. The chapter brings together a range of interviewing methods and modelling techniques whose origins range from counselling to methods for analysing qualitative data. We consider forms of mapping thinking that actively involve the problem-owner which we have been developing over the past seven years. Our objective is to convince you that understanding a problem as someone else sees it needs consideration and original methods for recording what you hear when you listen — to both verbal and non-verbal elements of a problem description.

Chapter 4 is a continuation of Chapter 3 and considers the technique we have developed and called 'cognitive mapping' as a method for modelling ideas, beliefs, and values. The map is an explicit basis for negotiation between the problem-helper and his client about the content and structure of his problem. It enables the explication and analysis of complex beliefs and values and is a working record of the problem as it changes and moves towards solution. The model-building technique can often be used by individuals to help themselves think about a problem. And it can be taken as the basis for the development of a numerically related model for analysis by the construction of computer simulation models which are understood by, and believable to, both the problem-owner and the helper. We shall be suggesting that cognitive mapping is a simple and effective technique for modelling and analysing a person's problem. We shall want you to see it as a sensible reflection of the arguments we shall have previously developed on the nature of organizations and the nature of problems, and to see it as a practical and yet a good reflection of the theory of decision-making.

Chapter 5 moves on to considering the situation of a problem-helper who is working with a team of individuals. A view of problems as personal, often idiosyncratic, constructions, set within an organizational context of internal politics and interpersonal relations, means that the problem-helper is confronted by a great deal of complexity. It means that he cannot treat the team as if it were a single individual with a single set of objectives and one problem definition. The likely existence of different objectives, different perspectives, and internal politics within a team means that the problem-helper will need to pay careful attention to thinking about, and negotiating, the nature of his intervention within a team. We shall also suggest that the problem-helper and team will be helped by methods of listening which facilitate holding on to and working with perhaps widely different interests and knowledge in a particular situation.

Chapter 6 expands this approach by looking at the way modelling can be used for creative problem-solving in teams. Cognitive maps can be used to keep hold of ideas as they arise in team meetings, to relate the ideas of one person to those of others and facilitate a jointly agreed problem definition. Our experience suggests that models of thinking which are constructed by a helper with all members of a team can be an extremely helpful method for sharing and checking assumptions, and for making creative use of individual experience and wisdom. We have been involved with groups who have wanted help in constructing imaginative possibilities for the future of their organization; a group wanting to devise and implement solutions to local unemployment; publishers wanting to create adventurous policies to sustain the editorial future of a magazine; probation officers wanting to manage their own team more effectively; a research team who felt they had problems of motivation; and with many other groups. In all these cases seeing problems as belonging to individuals, being set within a political arena, and as things needing careful listening using models have been the crucial elements in a successful team intervention. We shall attempt to show that the techniques and theories we have applied can be usefully set amongst behavioural science-based interventions where the management of interpersonal dynamics is the crucial element.

Chapter 7 represents a break from the type of material presented so far; we consider the relationship between modelling subjective and personal ideas and beliefs and mathematical modelling. In recent years the systems movement has been active in introducing approaches to the modelling of 'soft' systems but there is still a predominance of mathematically complex models published in the literature of Operational Research and Systems Analysis. We believe that there is much that can be achieved by blending the type of models we have discussed in the previous chapters with the need that often arises where a problem-owner wishes to go further into the numerical implications of his thinking. We introduce one of the methods (System Dynamics simulation modelling) that can be used to help the problem-owner follow the move from a model such as a cognitive map to a computer simulation model. Thus mathematical models can be set within qualitative considerations and built so that the problem-owner(s) feel committed to the results of the modelling activity. In this way the mathematical model and qualitative model enhance each other so that relevant problem solving help is provided.

After Chapter 8, the concluding chapter, we discuss in an appendix new computer software especially designed to help in the construction of cognitive maps, in their analysis, and in the merging of several maps into a single map. The software, which is written in FORTRAN, is essentially an extremely high-level language which can be used simply and interactively by the non-computer person. It represents many man-years of development and field testing and has the potential for bringing self-help in thinking about problems through the power of modern computing technology.

We have written the book so that it does not have to be read from cover to cover. The reader can stop at any point and be able to use the material he has read without relying on the subsequent chapters. What has been read can stand alone from what follows. For example, some managers may choose to stop after Chapter 3, project team leaders would probably want to read at least to Chapter 5, and so on. Some experience or grounding in mathematical modelling techniques will help in appreciating the significance of Chapter 8, although it does not require any mathematics to understand the contents. All readers might find the appendix on the use of computer software interesting and understandable whether or not they have read Chapter 6.

1
Distinct Perspectives
and Political Concerns

Consider the following account.

John Smith is a marketing manager in a division of a large manufacturing company, Ian Brown the division's newly appointed marketing director. John Smith had just been to a meeting of the marketing department, the first with its new director. The appointment had not been a great surprise. Most people had assumed that Ian would get the job after his predecessor Brian Jones had been promoted to Head Office. In the three years since he had joined the division, Ian's area had been particularly successful, with two major and successful new product launches. He also had exactly the right kind of personality, John mused, aggressive, dynamic, self-confident. Personally John did not like him and thought he could be an 'absolute bastard' at times, but John had to admit that he was good at his job. Furthermore, with the successor to Ian's old job still undecided it would be stupid to 'get on the wrong side' of the man, even if his own chances of getting the job were, at this stage, remote. Anyway, he thought, the meeting had not been the exciting event everyone had been expecting, although the fact that no announcements had been made about the successor would be bound to get everybody talking. In the meeting Ian had just gone over the future plans and there was nothing new, the usual policy statements about the fact that the division was strong in some markets, weak in others and efforts to find new products would continue to have a high priority.

Peter Williams, responsible for the industrial products section, had put forward his usual argument that the problems in his area had little to do with the division's (i.e. his) efforts and much more to do with overall adverse market conditions. There was no doubt that he was probably right and Ian had not openly disagreed, though he had cut Peter short in the middle of his 'spiel'. (Peter did tend to go on a bit.)

As John walked down the corridor Martin Evans, the promotions co-ordinator, came up to him. "What did you think of that, then?" he asked. "O.K.", John grunted, guardedly, turning into his office. Martin was one of those people he disliked and distrusted. His efforts to impress Ian in the meeting had been so obvious as to be almost amusing John thought.

As John sat down Alan Dixon came in. Alan was the new-products manager and a good friend both in and outside work. He was looking anxious. "Didn't like the sound of all that", he said. "I reckon we are all going to be under the microscope now. Did you notice how he looked at me when he said we should pay more attention to exploiting names in development? (John hadn't.) You know how much trouble I had convincing Brian that we should keep separate identities for products in different market segments. I thought I had won that one. Now it looks as if I'll have to go through it all over again. I tell you, if he starts trying to change things radically in my area, it will be a disaster. And what about the way he was getting at Peter? I think he is definitely going to try to give Peter the push. . . ."

THE INDIVIDUALITY OF REALITY

Although this scene is an imagined one, we hope that what it describes believably captures some of the flavour of organizational life as most of us experience it.

We left John and his friend Alan in the middle of discussing what had 'gone on' in the meeting they had both just attended. It is clear that Alan had placed an interpretation upon the events occurring in that meeting, in terms of potential significance for him, quite different from that belonging to John. His interpretation had led him to feel distinctly anxious about the future behaviour of the new marketing director. John, on the other hand, had found the meeting rather uneventful. We may even suppose that he had been disappointed that it had not been more exciting. Are we 'rigging' the story? Of course. Yet we would ask you to consider how often when 'comparing notes' with colleagues after a meeting you find that each person will recall different aspects of the meeting, place different emphases on different aspects, or interpret the implications of the meeting in different ways. Sometimes the differences can be so significant that it hardly seems that the same meeting is being discussed.

The point that we wish to make here is so obvious that it appears almost trivial. Different people interpret situations in different ways. We have much in common with others in our social worlds – language, shared beliefs about the nature of things and relationships between them, and shared norms about what we should or should not do. Many of these come to have a meaning so institutionalized that they are taken to be 'matters of fact'.[1] Nevertheless our individual histories are unique to each of us. Different people interpret situations in different ways because they bring to a situation their own particular mental 'framework' of

---

[1] For a detailed and important analysis of the relationship between 'subjective' and 'objective' realities and knowledge see Berger and Luckmann (1966). Another useful but difficult book in this context is by Silverman (1970) who describes and evaluates several different perspectives for understanding organizations, including his own orientation to the nature of actions as arising from the meaning individuals ascribe to events (see particularly Chapter 6).

personal beliefs, attitudes, hypotheses, prejudices, expectations, personal values and objectives, with which they can make sense of (place an interpretation upon) the situation.[2] Thus they pay attention to certain things, ignore others, and regard some as having a particular significance for themselves in the future.

Returning to our example, this perspective would lead us to suggest that different recollections of a meeting by different individuals, has less to do with one person having a 'better' memory than another than with how those individuals differently made sense of the meeting in terms of their particular mental frameworks. That is to say, individuals' recollections of a meeting and interpretations of what was significant within it come from their own beliefs and expectations — for example, about the world of things and people in general, about meetings in their organization, about the people there and their intentions — and from the future implications they see in the meeting for themselves in terms of their values and objectives.

These projected implications in turn lead to actions, or non-actions, to avoid undesirable consequences and move towards, or maintain, certain desired states of affairs that are a reflection of personal values and objectives. The 'model' of man we have and feel comfortable with is thus not of an organism responding to some 'stimulus', nor 'driven' by internal needs or instincts, nor of a person whose thinking and actions are socially 'given'. Rather it is of a human being who acts in the light of the personal interpretations or constructions he places upon events, in a process of 'scientific' enquiry about his reality so that it be, not a random unpredictable place, but one of order and meaning over which he may have some control.[3]

AN ORGANIZATION OF HUMAN BEINGS

Much of a person's hypothesizing about his world will be about the other human beings that make up that world. He will be concerned to understand what makes other people 'tick' as much as is enough for him to manage his interactions with them to his own satisfaction.

In the scenario described earlier we learned that John, the main protagonist, disliked his new boss but respected him for his competence, disliked and distrusted one of his colleagues and therefore avoided discussing his feelings about the meeting with him, but was involved in a close and friendly relationship with another who had dropped in immediately after the meeting for a 'post-mortem' on it. The point we wish to draw out here is that individuals in organizations are involved, as elsewhere, in complicated social relationships where they dislike,

---

[2] For a discussion of the nature of beliefs and values see Chapter 3 in Eden, Jones and Sims (1979). See also Young (1977) and Rokeach (1973).

[3] Our model of man is based significantly on the work of the cognitive psychologist Neisser (1976), the sociologists Thomas and Thomas' (1928) notion of 'defining the situation' and in particular Kelly's Theory of Personal Constructs (1955).

like, care about, find boring, are rude to, dismiss, fear, even fall in and out of love with, other members of the organizations. Much of their energy is spent in handling these relationships and in developing some understanding of those others in order to do so (and a large proportion of time is spent in, and enjoyment derived from, gossiping about other people).

So called 'irrationalities' of personal evaluations of other people as those who 'get up my nose' or 'bore the pants off me' have a great deal more influence on decisions which involve those people than perhaps we would care to admit. Thus, for example, we know that being liked by the boss is at least as important as being seen by him as competent, in terms of what we might be able to persuade him to do.[4] Most of the time our own behaviour and that of others is not reflected upon or managed in a particularly self-conscious way. We are usually as human beings extremely competent in dealing with all the nuances, variations, surprising twists and turns of interactions with other people. Brief discontinuities, moments of uncomfortableness in an otherwise satisfactory or, to us, unimportant relationship rarely represent serious problems for us.

However, there clearly are times when we see events in relationships with others as having significant implications that we do not like. Indeed there is a large body of professional practice concerned with teaching about, or intervening in, 'interpersonal' problems in organizations. Often it is assumed that there is some relatively straightforward demarcation between such 'interpersonal' problems and other kinds of problems. That such a demarcation is rarely, if ever, clear cut is one of the points we hope our example illustrates.

POLITICAL CONCERNS

John and his friend Alan had been ruminating about what Ian Brown, the new director, being the sort of man they believed him to be, and in the light of the things he had said in the meeting, might do in the future which would have implications for their life in the organization. In his new role Ian had suddenly become someone of much greater significance than in the past. The meeting had left Alan feeling anxious and we can readily imagine him spending no small amount of mental energy on attempting to predict exactly what Ian's future actions might be with respect to himself. He will probably attempt to 'suss' out the opinions and feelings of various colleagues. He will probably consider what strategies he might use to prevent Ian from interfering in ways that he does not like, and so on. We are touching here upon that category of activities in which individuals engage with respect to one another known as organizational politics. Specifically, self-consciously and according to some personal sense of a desired end to be served, they seek to gain other people's support for, or prevent them from hindering, certain states of affairs relating to those ends.

---

[4] For a discussion of the significance of personal relationships and what he terms 'particularism' in organizational decision-making see Perrow (1972).

To do this, individuals will seek to ensure that other people hold the definition of a situation that they want them to hold. They can do this in several ways. For example, they will sometimes attempt to persuade through the power of 'rational' argument, or through the self-evident merit of their image of desired ends or means, or by appeal to their own 'superior' expertise. Sometimes they will lie, cheat and attempt to manipulate. In either case they will be selective about what information they reveal and order its presentation in particular ways according to their own understanding of what is likely to be most persuasive to the particular people concerned. They will usually present their argument as reflecting a concern for the 'good' of the organization, or at least of those particular people. Often they will believe this to be so, sometimes they will not, but to admit otherwise would be to break one of the cardinal rules of the organizational political game – that of admitting to 'selfish' motives. The essence of this rule is not that people actually believe others to be unselfish, indeed usually quite the opposite. Simply that there appears to be an almost 'fact of the matter' norm among members of most organizations that it is illegitimate to admit to personal ends.

Because individuals with distinct perspectives and political concerns rarely reach complete agreement about ends and means, compromise outcomes are often negotiated or bargains struck about favours to be exchanged at different times.[5] Alliances will be formed, some relatively stable and enduring, others relatively short term. The energetic will spend considerable effort and time in finding out what others do want and think on a particular issue. (Often this involves a game-like process in which both parties know what is going on, are ready to be involved in what is going on, but do not acknowledge openly that they are participating in a lobbying process.) They will 'chat up' those they regard as powerful, not for any particular purpose but still with some strategic conception that such activities will bear fruit later in some particular context.[6] And they will do these things because they seek, as reasonable men and women, to pursue what they regard as right and best. It is important to be clear that organizational politics is not the sole territory of self-interested manipulators, megalomaniacs or charlatans.

THE CONTEXT FOR POLITICS

These activities are carried out within the context of the rules, procedures, norms, language and established structures of power within an organization,

---

[5] For an interesting analysis of the difficulty in distinguishing between means and ends in the pursuit of goals and objectives see Ackoff (1979).

[6] For a book which describes in detail the internal political aspects of organizational decision-making using the case study of the purchase of a computer see Pettigrew (1973). Another fascinating case is described, almost in the form of a novel, by Jones and Lakin (1978).

which serve to define the way things are done, the way to get things done, and often the way things 'just self-evidently are'. A successful political actor is usually one who knows the norms and the rules of his particular organizational game, some of which will be laid down in manuals, many of which are not. He will know which rules he must follow and which he can break through reference to another set.

Thus, for example, he will know that even if he is not unself-consciously a particularly energetic, assertive or decisive individual he should be seen to be so by 'the right people', if that is the valued persona in his particular organization. He will have learnt this by observing the behaviour of those who have received rewards in contrast to those who have tended to be ignored or 'punished', relating his observations to the language used to describe 'good' decision-makers, 'not so good' and 'bloody hopeless'. Often he will come to 'own' these bases for evaluation himself, as John had, in our example, unquestioningly appreciated Ian's 'go-getting' competence. If he is particularly effective he will adopt different personas with different groups at different times, but skilfully, to retain enough consistency that he is not likely to be branded as 'two-faced'.

He will know that he must present proposals within the language and the broad goal framework that top management have laid down as good for the organization, often themselves following what has gone before and become institutionalized as appropriate. He will have access to, if he is not already a part of, the powerful individuals and groups in the organization, either those who by virtue of their position have the power to reward or punish him, or those who themselves have significant contacts or influence networks – the committee secretary, the chairman's personal assistant (his wife?), the computer manager and so on.

The power that is exercised by these key actors is not always that coming from the potential of applying formal or informal sanctions. Often it is the power to 'write the agenda'. They may control and disseminate information in particular ways so as to reduce the likely perception of alternatives to what they regard as important and right. They may ensure that particular personnel selection policies are implemented. They may literally determine the agenda and order of business of meetings. Above all they may develop and reinforce procedures, rules, norms and language, resort to which then becomes the basis for rejecting certain proposals, accepting others and preventing some from ever being put forward.[7]

We have been painting a picture in which much of what goes on in organizations, including that which brings change, does so within a cultural framework

---

[7] See Lukes (1974) for an analysis of three dimensions of power including power which is exercised over people who do not even see alternatives to the current situation. Bachrach and Baratz (1970) is a classic text upon the power that is exercised through non-decision-making and the 'mobilization of bias'. Within the organizational context Pettigrew (1977) has also cogently described the 'management of meaning' as a crucial element in the organizational political process.

of rules, expectations and 'taken-for-granted' definitions of reality. Clearly, however, some individuals and groups can refuse to accept the rules, and if they can mobilize sufficient support, can change the nature of the game completely.[8]

Furthermore, to give the impression that we believe all individuals in all organizations are much of the time actively and energetically engaged in attempts to gain power of one kind or another would be a contradiction of our view of men as individuals, with their own frames of reference. Many people will view the organization simply as a means of providing them with a sufficient income to conduct what they regard as the most important parts of their lives outside the workplace.[9] Their politics extend no further than to ensure that they do not antagonize their boss, are doing a good enough job to ensure that they keep it, are promoted to a certain level according to their age. They are not interested in control over the direction and affairs of the organization.

Most of us move in several different social worlds and thus the pervasiveness of a particular world's definition of reality is usually, and fortunately, limited. Indeed, that we feel comfortable with the metaphor of organizational politics as a 'game', despite the fact that it is often deadly serious, is because so much of it involves rules and rituals that we know, in a meta-reflective way, are rules and rituals: "I know what I am doing and I know that you know that I know. . . ."

In any organization there are likely to be several different political 'games' between different groups of people and around different issues.[10] Some of these will overlap, as players are involved in several different games. Any individual interested in influencing particular events will need to decide which game (or games) is most important and appropriate for him to participate in. Being accepted as a credible player in an organizational political game, however, is a luxury (or curse) not open to everyone. A player in a management game may never be allowed into the internal political game on the shop floor, and vice versa. Even within what might be seen as their own 'circles' many do not occupy positions which give them entry to the appropriate networks of communication and power. Others still lack the personal skills of self-presentation, argument and negotiation that are, at least at a certain minimum level, necessary for being seen as a credible participant.

For those, however, who wish to have some control over what they are required to do in an organization, and over what certain others do, engaging in organizational politics is invariably essential. And while we, in the developed world, live in a society where social status, and often a personal sense of worth, is linked to the income and role titles which we derive from our occupation, then many

---

[8] See Mangham (1979) who argues strongly that it is possible to change the nature of the game.

[9] See Burns (1969).

[10] See the 'Governmental (bureaucratic) politics' paradigm in Allison (1971). In this book he lucidly illustrates how different 'conceptual spectacles' will lead you to look at and explain an organizational decision-making process in different ways.

of us will attempt to become involved in the competitive game of organizational politics by which we obtain these valued outcomes.

That we are prepared to make so many assertions about the nature of organizational life is because we believe that they are well founded in our own experience and the experience of others. Theoretically too, whether seeking to influence the affairs of men according to his own conception of what is right or best, or to defend his own freedom of action within a fairly limited area of influence, or to obtain the material and social rewards of particular positions, the individual who engages in organizational politics does so because he is a human being with his own goals, objectives, personal frame of reference. It is this 'individualistic' model of man which allows us to make certain generalizations about the pervasive nature of organizational politics.

IMPLICATIONS FOR PROBLEM-HELPING

The implications of the perspective on organizational life we have outlined here for thinking about problems and problem-helping methods will be explored in greater detail in the following chapters. Indeed the whole of this text is concerned with them in one way or another. However, we shall consider some of them briefly now.

To take this perspective seriously means that it is impossible to assume, self-evidently and non-problematically, that the way other people interpret a situation, is the same as, or even similar to, the way we interpret that 'same' situation. An event which you or I might see as a major crisis for a particular reason may be seen as a major crisis by someone else for completely different reasons, by another person as a minor difficulty, and yet other people may not even have noticed it at all. No situation is inherently, 'objectively' a problem. A problem belongs to a person; it is an often complicated, and always personal (albeit in some part shared with some others), construction that an individual places on events.

The construction which is a person's problem comes from a complicated mental framework of personal beliefs, attitudes, hypotheses, prejudices, expectations, objectives and values. Because people in organizations are involved in complicated social relationships, and frequently engage in internal political games of one kind or another, the way a person constructs a problem will also often include these aspects of their organizational life. Whether we disagree with, or regard as irrational, or illegitimate or stupid all these elements of a person's problem construction, they are his reality, and will be crucial to the choices he makes and actions he takes about his problems.

Thus, if one is attempting to find ways of helping people with their problems, statements such as "once we have found out what the real problem is we can solve it"; "yes, but as I see it the real problem is . . ."; "the problem with John is that he just does not understand the problem", hardly seem helpful. Yet they are more common than uncommon. They are unhelpful even when such statements are no more than a reflection of organizational culture and norms rather than a genuine intellectual commitment. They simply reinforce the other equally unhelpful but common features of the relationship between the helper and his 'client' which has to do with the mutual expectations of each other's role: the helper is a person who has techniques to help with the 'objective', 'rational', legitimate aspects of a problem (even if they are relatively insignificant to the client) and it is not only inappropriate, pointless, but potentially politically dangerous, for the client to move outside them.

Thereby the helper does not find out what is really bothering his clients. They work together on a problem which either neither of them, or just the helper 'owns'. In these circumstances often neither of them feels satisfied with the outcome, as, for example, when a helper works, with the best of intentions and effort, on a problem he thought his client had only to find out afterwards that his recommendations have been quietly ignored and the client is acting in ways that make no sense with respect to the problem the helper heard about; while the client, while acknowledging that the helper has done his best, is confirmed in his belief that the helper can only provide assistance with particular, and limited, aspects of problems.

During the past five years we have been developing and using with many different clients methods which can facilitate effective help to those who do not have nice, neat, 'rational', 'objective', legitimate and easily quantifiable problems. We do not argue that by means of them a helper will surmount all the difficulties of the helper—client relationship, set as it is within a context of organizational politics and the need for self-protection rather than openness. We do argue, however, that they can go some way towards reducing them and that if no attempt is made to move beyond techniques for neat and tidy or quantifiable or legitimate problems, then there will continue to be an important and unfortunate gap in the repertoire of problem-helping methods. The rest of this book describes, and sets in context, these methods.

Case Study

Ian Brown, the new marketing director of Leakey Products Ltd., was worried. He was anxious to get things moving, to make use of the ideas that he had had hanging around for a long time about the direction the company should be going; he was also keen not to let the grass grow under his feet because he felt that the easiest time to make most of the changes he wanted would be straight away. However, he was particularly concerned about Alan Dixon, the new product development manager. Alan, in Ian's opinion, was a highly competent and creative engineer, but Ian reckoned that the direction in which the competence and creativity were channelled might be the wrong one in the longer term. In fact everybody else around the department knew that Ian felt no enthusiasm for Alan's quest for the perfect tap.

Leakey Products Ltd., is an old established company which started off from manufacturing brass ball valves. Over the years it has expanded both into industrial taps and stop cocks, and with a range of bathroom and kitchen fittings. It was bought out by House Holdings Ltd., six years ago, and since then has developed the lines for which Ian had been responsible before his recent promotion, which were up-market taps and shower fittings.

Although the company had expanded, Ian felt that the industrial products division had been expanding less rapidly than the others, and he was convinced that there was a need for new products that reflected the directions of techno-logical change in the last few years. He felt that Alan, responsible for both consumer and industrial new-products development, had got out of touch with changes in market conditions in this area. Perhaps he was too interested in continuing technical improvements in taps, rather than in the new uses and control systems that had come in with the microchip. Alan, on the other hand, had already confided to John his feeling that "we are all going to be under the microscope now", which presumably meant that he felt that was where he was going to be. Alan was quite aware of Ian's attitude to his work, and felt it was unfair as he had been working long and hard to improve the performance of the company's products; for example his team had now produced a prototype valve for use with semi-fluids as well as having got most of Ian's product ideas off the ground. Some of Ian's ideas had been pretty impractical when Alan had taken them over. Alan had often had thoughts of moving to a new company where he could use his research and development talents more fully, but his wife and children are settled in the area and do not want to move. He is a professional engineer at heart – and proud of it.

So we see that Ian and Alan hold quite distinct perspectives on the 'new product' issue, each of these perspectives showing different political concerns. Meanwhile John and Peter, who occupy two of the three marketing manager posts (Ian's old job has yet to be filled), are not giving thought to the 'new product' issue – they have enough worries trying to meet their targets and prepare themselves for any attempts by Ian to change their budgets and staffing levels. The distinct perspective of John and Peter is that they do not feel they have any particular perspective or political concern about new products.

Within this context Ian decides that the best way of coping with Alan is to tell him to freeze all current product development projects and ask him to prepare a full analysis of the future both for existing products and for new product opportunities in the light of a detailed forecast of market opportunities. The marketing department does not have a resident mathematician/statistician and so Ian thinks it would be helpful to enlist the help of a Central Services consultant. The more he thought about it, the more enthusiastic Ian became about involving an outside consultant because he believed that having a scientist work with Alan might help convince him of the 'misguidedness' of his current work, and encourage Alan to develop in a fruitful way for the long-term success of the marketing operation.

But what are the prospects for the consultant from Central Services in entering such a situation? How will someone from Head Office cope with such a mess of different needs and such a maze of potential clients? Will Alan co-operate with the internal consultant or will he keep giving her duff data? Can John and Peter show any interest at all? Is the consultant going to be constrained to a routine piece of statistical sales forecasting, or can she find a way (if she wishes to do so) of making sense of the distinct perspectives, ideas, and political concerns?

2

Helping with Problems

The last chapter ended with some statements about the implications of the nature of problems for the practice of helping people in organizations. This chapter will go in greater detail into the individual way that people see problems, and the consequences this has for those who wish to give or receive help over problems. Most helpers see themselves as being in business either to solve problems for their clients or to help their clients solve their own problems. But what are problems?[1]

We usually refer to ourselves as having a problem if things are not as we would like them to be, and we are not quite sure what to do about it. If this chapter is coming out in a way which we think will not be quite clear to a reader, and we want it to be clear to the reader, and we do not know how to go about making it clearer, we have a problem. If we know how to do it but just have not got round to it yet, we would not usually dignify our dilatoriness with the word 'problem'; similarly if we reckoned it was going to be difficult for us to get the chapter right, but quite possible if we put the effort in, then that too would not usually be described by us as 'a problem'. If we were perplexed about this chapter, and did not feel it was quite right, but did not know what to do about it, then that is the sort of thing that we describe as a problem.

One of the most frustrating things often about knowing that something is not quite as we would wish but not knowing what to do about it is that if someone asks us – or we ask ourselves – "What is the problem?", we do not really know the answer to that question. If the person who asks us is our boss, a friend of our boss, someone who is competing with us for the next promotion, or someone who works for us and we are not quite sure what they think of us, then we might present one label. If it was someone we knew and trusted, we might present another label. In any case, how you answer the question "What is the problem?" depends on who you are talking to, if only because you expect different people to be able to understand different things. So if you are talking to someone with the intention of helping them with some problem, the description you get on the problem may vary a lot with how they see you.

We can usually give some sort of answer to the question "What is the problem?", but it may not be an answer that convinces us, and we often feel we have only

[1] For further discussion of this question, see Eden and Sims (1979) and Sims (1978, 1979).

12

been able to give a rather limited description. So it is quite common that the only descriptions we can find for problems are, without in any way being intended to be lies, not descriptions that we feel contain the most important truths about our problems.

Now this is a common feature of the experience of many people, that the step between feeling some sort of discomfort or dissatisfaction, feeling that there is some problem somewhere, and being able to say "The problem is such-and-such" is a very big step. In fact quite often we find that if we can say what the problem is we have gone a long way towards solving it. This seems to be true with any kind of problem, whether it be some technically oriented work problem, a relationship problem at home, or anything in between.

One of the properties of problems with which helpers have found it quite hard to grapple is the extent to which all problems are personal; different persons see different problems in what other people would take to be the same situation. This is an important point in our argument, and it is fairly well accepted in everyday 'common sense'. This point does not seem to raise much disagreement when it is expressed theoretically, but it is often rather more difficult to bear it in mind and act upon it in practice. For this reason, we shall give three examples of what different people seeing different problems may look like.

Suppose that a student reported himself as feeling tired and listless, generally not very well, and that he did not feel he could be bothered to do anything. A students' union officer might conclude that the student's problem was depression, and might probe to find out more about the depression by asking the student how long it had been going on. The doctor at the University medical centre might say that the problem was a cold, that there were a lot of them about and that she had just had one herself. The student's academic tutor might think that the student was not absorbing himself sufficiently in his work, and that a bit more application and hard work would make still more application and hard work easier. The campus radical might think that the problem was classical anomie and alienation, brought on by the death throes of the capitalist system, and the student counsellor might start from the belief that the problem must lie with the student's sex life. Each of these people finds a different problem in the situation, at least in part because they are each inclined to attribute different causes to events.

For another example, think of a board of directors in a medium-sized manufacturing firm, confronted with a set of figures which show that they 'have a problem of' their market share declining. In this case, the people involved might agree this label for their problem, but might have quite different interpretations of that agreed problem label. The production director may think that the problem is a hopeless advertising campaign that the marketing department have bought, the marketing director may think that the problem is the inflexibility of the production department, which prevents them from being able to offer customers the delivery dates and special options that competitors can achieve. The finance director may think that the problem is excessive conservatism on the part of both the marketing and the production directors in continuing with rigid quality control even though it means that their product is a little more expensive than others on the market.

It is by no means always the case that people assume that problems stem from others rather than themselves. For example, on a magazine, it would be quite possible for an editor to think that they are losing readers because the features editor has become fascinated by some subject which bores most of their readers, while the advertisement controller may attribute loss of readers to a decrease in the number of advertising pages. Both people might believe that it is really their contribution that the magazine depends on, and so any serious problems must stem from their own function.

When we talk about problems, we are not necessarily thinking of problems in the negative sense – our definition was that a problem was a situation where someone wanted something to be different from how it was and was not quite sure how to go about making it so. Thus opportunities for building on strengths and making positive improvements, openings that you feel are there to be exploited but you cannot quite see how at the moment, are also counted as problems for our purpose. The same point about how different people see different problems still applies. The editor and the advertisement controller of a successful magazine may well see different problems in the sense of different opportunities for their magazine, where the editor may think that there is an opportunity to expand the editorial content by a few pages, and thus bring in large numbers of extra readers, ensuring the health, future and profitability of the magazine. The advertisement controller may at the same time see an opportunity to tie the editorial matter more closely to the advertising material, and increase the number of pages of prestige advertising, thus enabling them to increase the rate per page for advertising there, and so ensuring the health, future and profitability of the magazine!

So different people see different problems, and in this sense problems are made and not born. To some extent we believe we can generalize about the kinds of problems that people of different roles, personalities and cultures define for themselves. For example, there is a frequent generalization in the Health Service that, while physicians see everything (not just patients) as complicated and needing a lot of thought, surgeons see all problems as much more cut and dried (*sic*). Some personalities seem to find the running of a large business to be something which they just get on with and which they do not see as problematic, while others find it a very difficult problem to decide what to eat for lunch. In some cultures, possession of a certain kind of problem seems to be very important to people. For some people in British engineering companies, for example, to have no problem of stress and overworking suggests to them that they are slacking, or unimportant, or in some other way deficient. With some people it seems that if they are short of problems at work they manage to devise themselves the most amazingly complicated problems to do with how they go on holiday.

All these differences in the kinds of problem that different people see do not necessarily imply that any of them are wrong, or that they are deceiving themselves, but rather that almost any situation that a person might be dissatisfied with can be seen as having multiple causes, and any one of those causes may be taken as the central point to hang a problem around. If a person is dissatisfied with the amount of money they have, they may say that the problem is too much taxation, or that their company pays them too little, or that their financial aspirations are too high, or any of a huge number of possible tags that could be used to describe the problem that they are experiencing. They may say all of these things, and mean them, which means that it is very important not to take the first verbal tag offered as being 'the problem', but only as an initial indicator that there may be a complicated interlocking mess of problems there to be investigated.[2]

When we are in a situation which is complex and worrying, we are usually too busy and too anxious and too involved with that situation to perceive such choices of what we might see the problem as being; they are often visible only from the outside. Because most of us have experienced this many times over the years, we have some experience of recognizing our own state of anxiety and asking some other person for the kind of help that we want. Often the most helpful thing that others do for us can be to make some suggestion, or put forward some idea, which enables us to change our problem. This is also, however, the most easily rejected form of help. If we do not 'own' the problem that the would-be helper is offering us, then we will not be interested in working on it; it is quite easy to reject the sort of help which starts from trying to tell us that our problem is not 'really' what we thought it was. Usually, if we ask someone for help with some situation that is worrying us, the relationship between us and that person is already quite close, so that we can predict and control the kind of help we get. The professional 'helper' in an organization, however, has often to work within a less-developed relationship with those who are being helped, who do not know the helper well enough to feel confident that they can defend themselves against his help.

THE HELPER AND PROBLEMS

Problems, then, are very individual things in the sense that different persons might see quite different problems in the same situation. The individual may find it helpful to remember that another person might construct a quite different

---

[2] The idea of problems being found in 'messes' comes from Ackoff (1974, p. 4), who describes a mess as a 'system of problems'. Kepner and Tregoe (1965, p. 63) use a different definition of mess, very similar to our definition of 'problem'.

problem, or even no problem at all, if they were in the same situation; this fact may be of some help in letting a person think more laterally about their problems.

The argument becomes much more significant, however, when we think about problems with which several persons are concerned, because in that case those persons might have quite different views of the problem, both because they have different ways of understanding what is going on around them, and also possibly because they have different interests, responsibilities, duties and relationships, which lead them to quite different concerns. In the cases that interest us, for helping with problems, there must always be at least two persons involved — the helper and the client. It is very rarely as few as that, however. It would not be untypical in an organization for a person to feel unease or disquiet about something, and for them then to need the agreement of their colleagues and their boss before they can talk to a helper about it. When they talk to their colleagues and boss, they will almost certainly have to answer questions from them about "What is the problem?" They will need to give them some answer to that question, which shows that the problem is of a type that they need help with, but which also does not suggest that they need help because they are incompetent (presuming they do not want to be thought incompetent), and also probably which suggests to them that it is in their interests too to have help with this problem; so the person might well choose to state their problem in a way that implies that a solution to it might also solve problems that they suspect some of their colleagues have. They will also almost invariably feel the need to talk about this problem in terms of not being satisfied over the things that are publicly regarded in their organization as legitimate values; this means that a lot of problems which might initially have had nothing to do with such concepts end up being talked about in the teams of the persons who have them in terms of profit, efficiency, ensuring future markets and so on. Even within a team of managers who get on reasonably well and trust each other, it would be unusual for a problem to be phrased in more personal and less legitimate terms such as promotion, making life easier for oneself, or gaining some advantage over another department in the organization.

Not only will the person who introduces the problem produce a carefully doctored version in this way, but also the other members of the team will want to have their say, and so produce further and possibly drastic changes, as the problem is discussed and negotiated within the team. Once again, the points they make are edited by them in line with years of hard-earned and successful experience in that organization, as to what sort of things they need to say in order to get what they want and maintain a favourable image with one another. The skills which all of us who work in organizations develop mean that, without anyone being in the least untruthful or deliberately deceitful, the discussion is almost bound to be quite some way removed from a frank and open discussion of what it is that is eating us.

Now the whole process of careful and selective presentation of the problem happens once again. Whoever it is who has the right or the duty to talk to a helper about it and to become 'the client' presents that problem in a way that they hope is clear enough to enable the helper to do something helpful. At the same time, they describe the problem in a way which does not present themselves or their colleagues in too bad a light, and which they do not think will lead to the helper making recommendations that are against their interests as they see them. Depending on the structure and the division of responsibilities within the client organization, the person who presents the problem to a helper may or may not be the person who originally felt some discomfort or unease. In either case, the problem has undergone an enormous amount of restating and editing between the original feeling of discomfort by a person and the version that gets related to a helper. Similar changes, selection, forgetting of some parts and emphasis of other parts can be expected again where the helper is part of a team of helpers rather than a solitary individual. All this, it should be noted, presumes good will and no intention to mislead on the part of anybody. We are for the moment ignoring such situations as when a person presents a problem which they intend to lead to the downfall and removal of one of their colleagues, or where someone lays claim to a problem which they do not actually feel, but they think will impress their colleagues, or where a helper is brought in to talk about a problem in the hope that they will fail, so that the problem concerned can be shown to be of huge proportions and unassailable. A current favourite is to put a problem to a helper in such a way that you get a report back from him which can then be argued as a case for making people redundant; "we deeply regret this, but the study that has been carried out by independent consultants has shown that . . .", and the helper, by being set a carefully selected problem, has produced a predictable answer which can then be used by the clients as a pseudo-objective justification for the action they were going to take anyhow.

For another example, two departments in an oil company both retained Operational Research consultants to look at the question of how much storage tankage should be built at a particular refinery. Both groups set out to produce profit-maximizing answers to the question. Each group was given the context of the issue by its employing department, and both groups came up with answers which were in the interests of their department; the two answers conflicted sharply. Even in this case, it seems unlikely that the persons concerned thought they were distorting anything. Much more likely is that they thought they were giving the 'right' description of the problem. So how does a helper begin to be helpful in such a complicated situation?

The first answer to this question that we have found useful is to find ways to help clients to talk as directly as they can about what it is that is concerning them. If the helper is labelled as an Operational Researcher, clients may feel that they should quantify as much as they can of what they say to him. Nothing wrong with that, of course, if they were already thinking of it all quantitatively, but quite often they may not have been doing so, the quantities they give may be an afterthought; they do not feel very confident in the quantification, and therefore however good the rest of the helper–client interaction, they will not feel very confident in the outcome of whatever work the helper does. They know that it was all based on doubtful data in the first place. So it is important that the client should feel able to talk about things in non-quantitative ways.

Similarly, a lot of factors that are significant in many of the more important organizational decisions are not seen by the decision-maker as being definite points, but rather are feelings, or hunches, or theories. When talking to helpers they are quite likely to feel that they should not spend their time telling a 'management scientist' about feelings and theories, but should rather stick to the 'facts'. It is our experience that the things that are seen as objective, hard 'facts' around problems that are really concerning people are often fairly trivial compared with the subjective, soft 'feelings' or 'theories' that they see as central to it. This is scarcely surprising, because people who are dealing with complicated and large issues will have built up a body of experience and wisdom over time which probably incorporates more different things than they would know how to separate out or talk about; their 'feelings' are actually based on a huge number of 'facts', but because they cannot remember and describe those facts individually, they may not regard the resulting feeling as a worthy topic to talk about in front of a helper. Helpers who let such an inhibition persist will be deprived of most of their clients' important thinking about their situations.

Again, whether or not the helper likes the values, the personal goals and the organizational politics being pursued by the client, they do not go away or become less potent for the client by being ignored by the helper. Helpers who do not wish to blindfold themselves while serving the client will find that they can serve both themselves and the client better to the extent that these matters can be brought into the open between them. Helpers are likely to be more useful if they know what they are doing.

STYLES OF HELP

The second group of points that we would make about the sort of complexities that we have been describing in talking about problems between helper and client have to do with three different approaches to giving help.[3]

Firstly, we can recognize a 'coercive' approach. By this we mean that helpers may use some of their power to tell the client what problem they think the client ought to have and ought to be working on. If helpers present themselves as experts, and clients accept them as such, that means that the helpers will have some power to tell the clients what they ought to think.

Coercive strategies are very rarely completely open, but are more likely to take the form of name dropping, either about techniques or skills that the helper

---

[3] For more detailed discussion of these approaches to giving help, see Eden and Sims (1979).

has, or about powerfully placed persons in the organization with whom the helper claims to have links. Because a complicated view of a situation tends to be a bit cumbersome, it often happens that a simpler view can drive out a more complicated one, and this also enables helpers coercively to introduce their own definitions of a problem, simply because they do not know so much about what is going on. Few helpers would acknowledge that they coerce their clients into having particular problems, but an awful lot are prepared to admit that in particular cases they did use some fairly heavy forms of influence. Coercion is not necessarily a one-way process, either. A client who is exceedingly deferential, exhibits great confusion, and begs the helper for their 'objective' view, is going a long way towards coercing the helper into taking a coercive stance.

Secondly, we can recognize an empathetic approach. In this approach, the helper attempts to understand fully the client's problem, and to stay within the client's way of understanding things and taking action. Many schools of consultancy advise their adherents to 'start from where the client is', or that the consultant should only work on the problem that the client sees. In this case, the helper attempts to reflect back to the client what they are saying, and is careful not to make suggestions – because such suggestions would belong not to the client but to the helper. This approach has a drawback in that, ultimately, no person can fully understand another person's problem without becoming that person; and if they could become that person, not only would they understand that problem, but they would have it.

A third approach to giving help is what we call a 'negotiative' approach, by which we mean that, instead of taking either the helper's definition of the problem and working on that, as in the coercive approach, or being confined to the client's definition of the problem, as in the empathetic approach, the helper should reckon on having a period of negotiation with the client. This will start from empathetic listening by the helper to what the client has to say about a problem. They then proceed to negotiate a problem which both can become interested in and committed to, the solution of which will fulfil needs for both of them, even though it is unlikely to be either strictly the felt problem of the client, or a problem which the helper comes in thinking would be a good one to look at. By aiming to operate within this paradigm, helpers are acknowledging that what they do with their clients in arriving at a problem is similar to what their clients do among themselves in their teams in arriving at a description of the problem they are prepared to give to a helper. To the extent that helpers acknowledge that this is what is going on, they and their clients can be more aware and deliberate in what they do.

This avoids some of the drawbacks of the coercive approach, where it is quite easy for a helper to produce and possibly even to implement elegant solutions to problems that nobody had anyhow, or for a helper to feel that they have something to say, and then to find that the client does not seem to listen to them (any more than they listened to the client). It also avoids some of the drawbacks of the empathetic approach, which demands a superhuman achievement from the helper in listening to and understanding the felt problems of their clients. We say superhuman because the helper is a different person with different values, needs and interests, and is therefore very unlikely to be able to feel precisely the problem that the client feels when inhabiting a situation. Life is too short for the client to tell the helper all the ramifications of their problem, and why and how they feel it as a problem, and what its context is. In the negotiative approach it is still very important for helpers to start by listening to and empathizing with their clients, so that they can understand the meaning of what the client tells them, and because this is likely to set the tone for more understanding in both directions. What happens from then on, however, is not the same as in the empathetic approach.

In this chapter we have outlined a number of overall directions that we think make for effective helping with problems. The recommendations, however, remain as empty theorizing without a technique to help a person become both more capable of addressing problems in the form in which they matter to their clients, that is, with not many constraints on problem formulation, and also capable of managing explicitly a negotiative approach for finding the problems to help with. We shall go on in Chapters 3 and 4 to look at techniques which make these ideas easier to operate. Before that, however, we should say a little bit about help that is and is not helpful.

ENABLING AND DISABLING HELP

Some of the United Nations organizations taught their members to be wary about assuming the role of helper with the fable of the monkey in the flood, which goes roughly like this.

A monkey was sitting in his favourite tree in the forest during a sudden flood. Seeing a lot of his fellow creatures being swept away in the flood, and being a helpful monkey, he kept reaching out his long arm into the flood waters and rescuing passing creatures, which he pulled out and put in a large flat part in a fork in the boughs of the tree. The little brown things with four legs and with or without fur were mostly grateful to the monkey, but the oblong silver things with big mouths seemed upset. In fact the silver things all died, but the monkey assumed that this was because they had been in the water too long, and his help had come too late. He did not understand why it was that the fish were not grateful for his technical 'assistance'.

It often does not feel much more helpful than this if someone comes to your aid when things are getting difficult in a meeting. However helpful the intentions of the would-be helper, it is very difficult for the helped not to find themselves defined in the eyes of everybody else around as incompetent by the very fact that someone helped them and therefore they obviously needed help. Try helping some stutterers to finish their sentence, or some children to finish their jigsaw puzzle if the idea that help is not always seen as helpful needs any more demonstration. Most people who have ever had a helpful boss agree that there were things that they just never learned to do for themselves, so long as help was available from that boss. Intendedly helpful feedback about how we are performing in our work may be anything from celestial to abysmal according to who gives it to whom, with what intent, and according to the care with which the helpers identify and restrict themselves to the help that the helped can cope with. Some people sometimes feel that they have got problems enough of their own without having to cope and negotiate with someone helping them with them as well (negotiative approach). It may also be unhelpful to have a deeply concerned helper becoming thoroughly involved in your problems (empathetic approach), or to have a clear-thinking expert doing incomprehensible calculations and manipulations on their simplified version of your problems (coercive approach).

We have argued that in some cases problems can be quite private possessions, quite personal things, and it has been said that in some cases to solve a person's problems may be nothing short of robbery.[4] What may be a problem to one person may be a part of their identity in their working world to another.

It seems to us that any approach to helping has the potential to disable as well as to enable. A particularly common cause of disabling help is inadequate listening by the helper to the client. The half-attentive listening of most social interaction is because much of the listener's attention is taken up with planning their next sentence or considering what impression they are making. Such listening may well keep the relationship between helper and client sweet, but is most unlikely to lead to enabling help. Attentive listening needs to be positively practised, and we shall be offering techniques in the next chapter that help with this.

We have said that client expectations may coerce a helper into a coercive approach. If this permits the client to become dependent on the helper, this could be disabling if the helper is not prepared to support the client's dependency. Such dependency is too important, and too potentially damaging, to be safely slipped into unawares, and is worth considering explicitly as part of the problem by the parties. Sigmund Freud suggested that it might be helpful to offer clients (or in his case, patients) solutions to their problems; if they disagree with these solutions, that disagreement might help to clarify their thoughts. This is a justification for what many helpers do anyhow. We would be very reluctant to use such an approach, except with clients who knew us very well, because of the possibility of creeping dependency. Otherwise, the client may feel that the only options are either to accept the solution, or to reject both the solution and the helper who offered it.

---

4 This point is well made by Cook (1976, p. 8).

Case Study

Jenny Horse had been an internal consultant at Head Office for the last couple of years, before which she had been in a similar position in a chemical company. She had visited some of the operating companies of House Holdings Ltd. quite a few times, but had only been to Leakey Products once, so she was quite pleased when her boss said to her one morning; "Ian Brown, the marketing director of Leakey, has asked us whether we can do a sales forecast for him. The situation seems to be that he wants a model of what's going on in the market and they don't have anyone who can do that sort of thing." "It's probably fairly routine stuff but try to stay with it; Ian Brown is a bit of a high-flyer and there might be more work in the future. He's probably worth knowing as a political ally."

Under grey skies Jenny drove to meet Ian. On the way she pondered on what she knew of the project – the marketing managers usually do the sales forecasts, what were they going to think about her repeating the exercise, albeit with the help of statistical packages? Last time she was at Leakey they hadn't seemed too keen on Head Office involvement (but that had been a project instigated by Head Office).

Ian turned up half an hour late apologizing profusely – it seemed the typical start to a project!

After the usual palaver he launched into an explanation of why he wanted her involved. "We need an outsider's view. I think we're not really up to date with how the market's working. Although my marketing managers do annual forecasts for budgeting and targeting purposes we now need a more sophisticated analysis of our markets. I gather your group have done some good market modelling. What I want is something to help us consider new product development strategies."

Ian went on to give her some of the background to the company's products and tell her who his senior managers were. "I would like you to involve Alan, the new-products development manager, in your work. I realize you will need to liaise with the marketing managers but can you let Alan know what you're doing. I hope that he can learn about your approach and get a feel for the data and its implications."

At this point we note that the issue Ian is presenting is beginning to change its form. The issue has been edited so that it looks legitimate as something to talk to Jenny about, although Ian has obliquely indicated that he is dissatisfied with the way new-products development is done. Ian has role expectations of Jenny and presents those aspects of his issue that meet those expectations.

Jenny left Leakey feeling that she could handle the job but registering a need to spend longer with Ian to get a better idea of what sort of report he wanted. She and her boss cobbled together some project terms of reference that would enable the project to get started. Four weeks had been allowed for getting an initial model design for Ian to see. Jenny's boss was very keen on leaving terms of reference open enough for the nature of the project to change if necessary so that his staff could help the client as needed. Thus quite reasonably he was allowing them to define and redefine the issue as they learned about it. Sometimes this made for problems in establishing a budget for the project, but this was usually managed by laying down clear review dates. Ian was happy with this arrangement and wanted Jenny to start as soon as possible.

At the back of Jenny's mind was a nagging doubt that there was something too neat about the problem that Ian had been telling her about. He had told her what he wanted to know about, who the staff involved were, and it had all sounded like a nice, clean, sanitary sort of place in which to do a careful piece of modelling. But where was that smell coming from? The things that Ian had said about wanting Alan involved – what did they amount to? It had sounded all right at the time, and Jenny had not wanted to annoy Ian by going into minute detail about everything he said; after all, he was very much her senior, and she knew that her boss was keen that they should do more work with Leakey. In the past most of the consultancy work in Leakey had been done by the systems group from the accounts department at Head Office – in Jenny's eyes, a group that tended to go round telling their clients what problems to have, which she didn't think led to a particularly helpful and productive client–consultant relationship.

So Jenny had held off challenging too much why Ian wanted Alan involved, and, for all she knew, maybe the work for the new-products manager was connected with the marketing managers in a way that would make sense of such an involvement. By now she was kicking herself for not having gone a bit further on this during her initial meeting. She felt that she could probably have done more to encourage Ian to talk rather more to her and rather less to his stereotype of a model builder from Head Office. What was he up to? She had once been sent down to Rubber Washers Division to build a model, which everybody there had been very helpful about, and which had then been used by the management as a justification for closing the Division and buying in washers instead; ever since then Jenny had been reluctant to work without having some fairly clear idea about what her clients were trying to get out of what she was doing.

Not that she thought Ian was necessarily pulling a fast one. It was equally likely that he had not felt able to tell her all that much at a first meeting, and had had to make it all sound fairly respectable for the consultant from Head Office. But she knew that if it continued being that respectable, she would probably not end up being all that helpful. For all she knew, it might well not have been Ian who felt concerned in the first place.

The following day it seemed a lot clearer to Jenny. She would ring Alan and fix a time to go and see him, because she felt she needed to learn a bit about how Alan felt about the issue before she went any further. Would he, for example, feel threatened by her coming in as an outsider, when it was so unclear about how what she was doing related to his field? Afterwards, if possible, she would go and have a chat with one of the marketing managers; it would make less of a thing of her visit to Alan if she were seeing one of the others too, and the last thing she wanted to do was to start solving problems that nobody else thought existed, because she knew from bitter experience that problems would probably be created if she did. Also, to see one of the marketing managers at the same time would kill two birds with one stone.

She thought perhaps John would be a good one to start with; he sounded from what Ian had said as if he would be quite interested and quite ready to talk. But could she do that before seeing Ian again? Probably not — she was not sure yet exactly what she would be talking to Alan and John about. So she picked up the telephone and rang Ian. His secretary (what was her name — she must try and make friends with her if she was going to be able to get hold of Ian when necessary) said that he was away till the end of the week, and was really hopelessly busy next week. So she tried Alan instead. He was a bit surprised to hear from her, but Ian had mentioned that she would be around some time. Yes, he could see her the following Monday in the afternoon. So Jenny told him that she was wanting to talk to John as well, afterwards, if possible. "I'll see what we can do" said Alan, "John's right here in my office. I'll pass you over to him." John said he was tied up in a meeting all afternoon, but would be free at lunch time, and could have a chat with Jenny then. But who was she? Because if she was coming to look at the office supervisor's job, he was not at all the person to ask about it, and anyhow he felt it was only fair to admit that he thought it was a mistake to promote somebody from Head Office. Jenny tried to give a brief description of what she was coming down for, but felt very much at a disadvantage with talking to someone who was on the telephone in somebody else's office, and also felt that she had got off on the wrong foot. But she had her two appointments for next week.

3

Helping Clients Talk about Their Problems

In the previous chapter we have argued that problems belong to people and are not objective entities. If this is the case then we are totally dependent upon the client being able to tell us about his problem if we are to be able effectively to help him, or manipulate him to our own point of view. The starting point for working with problems is, idealistically, an empathetic understanding of the problem as the client sees it. One of the most powerful ways of achieving some empathy is through the careful act of listening to the language, descriptions, theories and beliefs that are expressed during introductory discussions with the client. Listening in this way is not an activity which can be undertaken in the everyday sense the word implies, but rather it demands well-developed skills and a great deal of concentration. The description of the problem, as it is heard by the problem-helper, is the basis for model building, analysis, negotiation and help as the problem which is constructed from initial listening is negotiated into a form explicit to both client and helper and to which both feel a sense of ownership.

However, it seems all very well to argue that a helper should listen carefully to the problem as the client sees it; but what if the client finds it difficult to articulate his concerns? The previous chapters mentioned some of the reasons why this may be so. Those that are most often given are to do with the 'politics of helping' in organizations and to do with client–helper expectations. The client does not want to declare particular aspects of the problem to someone from another department, or to declare concerns which seem to him to be personal rather than 'organizational'. The client reckons that the helper is a number cruncher and therefore will not be interested in the more evaluative and qualitative aspects of the problem, so he talks only about those aspects which he believes to be amenable to number crunching. Whatever expectations both persons have about one another's role they will both usually see constraints which derive from the culture of the organization about how problems are described. There is another reason which many helpers often come across – and that is the client quite simply finds it difficult to find the words which satisfactorily express his concerns.

This chapter is about a number of techniques which we have found helpful to both client and helper in making the problem explicit to both of them so that each is understanding mostly the same view of the problem. None of the techniques is the best or worst, their usefulness will be contingent on the particular circumstances of the problem-solving activity. Neither should they be regarded as separate strategies, they are amenable to being appropriately synthesized into an approach which suits your own style and inclinations.

Any techniques which have been helpful in facilitating problem construction between problem-owner and -helper are also likely to be useful when a person wishes to collect the idiosyncratic views of individuals in a group. We have often used the following techniques, or variations of them, when we have been concerned to involve several members of a project team in constructing a 'group problem'. Alternatively we have found them useful for encouraging participation when apathy has been prevalent and the client has wanted greater involvement from his 'team'.

The techniques are not introduced in any special order and are collected together in one chapter mostly because they pan out to a sensible chapter length. Thus Chapter 4, which considers specifically 'cognitive mapping', should be treated as a continuation of this chapter in that its purpose is the same.

RAMBLING

Probably the most obvious method for getting to know about the view a person has of a problem is to give him the time and space to 'ramble' around his subject. This can be an enormous strain on the listener for it is difficult to concentrate and difficult not to interrupt. The client will wander down several alleys that seem to bear little relationship to the problem as it was labelled at the start. Nevertheless by concentrating on collecting impressions of the more general parts of the client's 'world-taken-for-granted' it will be possible to see something of what he sees and to discover something about the spectacles through which he makes sense of people and events. In the same way as interrogation methods often depend upon allowing the prisoner to ramble so that they inevitably give away 'too much' of themselves, it seems possible that if the helper simply gives a client time and space then he will manage to communicate much of his problem.

Although it is not the most usual circumstance, there are times when the client is pleased to ramble freely. It seems to be more usual for the client to have some difficulty in stating his problem. Often we may conclude that if a problem can be stated easily then it is not much of a problem and probably doesn't need the help of a consultant — characteristically problems are confusing, unclear and difficult to state in a way which seems to capture them adequately. Clients often feel an immense sense of frustration after describing a problem, for it sounds to be simple but he knows this not to be the case, it has just not been possible to tell it as it feels.

A significant disadvantage, for the helper, of having a client talk openly and freely is that the helper thinks he knows 'what it's all about' rather too quickly and consequently moves to the negotiation part of problem construction without understanding the problem. How often have you experienced a friend or colleague hear you talk about a problem and quickly see it as simple and so offer solutions? Implicitly such interactions demonstrate arrogance on the part of the helper by their implied suggestion of stupidity on your part. This is, of course, not always the case, for sometimes a friend can 'see the wood from the trees'. But the danger is still large enough to care about — the operational researcher, for example, stands a good chance of presuming he knows the client's problem from 'terms of reference' and then going away from the client to solve it — as if to suggest that the direct experience and involvement of being the decision-maker is to be discounted in the problem-solving!

When you feel confident you 'know' what the client is talking about and feel intuitively confident about the imaginative leaps you make to save time in problem construction, then is the time to be wary. Most persons' experience of being on the end of such confident helpfulness is that they 'only wish he'd just listen for a minute'. Such confident help is characteristic of the sort of 'disabling help' we referred to in the previous chapter. Our experience in these circumstances suggests that the helper must take more than usual care to discipline his early role to that of 'empathetic' listener rather than pseudo-empathetic activist.[1]

Once talking freely, the client is not likely to need structured encouragement to discuss his problem. The effective role for the consultant, at this early stage, is that of passive listener — in the sense of being non-evaluative, actively modelling what is being said, and trying to discern the significant groups of ideas that each signal a problem within the client's 'mess'.

The sense of passivity captured in the last sentence is important, for passivity does not mean giving no feedback of any sort — the client will be likely to think you're bored, thinking about something else, can't understand a word that he's saying, and so on. This will particularly be the case if he is himself confused and bothered about the whole event. Thus it is important to present some feedback — for example, non-verbals such as nodding, saying "I see", etc.

ANOTHER ASPECT OF EMPATHY

Films, television and Woody Allen have introduced us all to stereotypical images of the American psycho-analyst. One of the projected features of the activity of the analyst is the apparent 'nothingness' contained in his vocal interventions. The analyst seems to merely repeat back to the client what has just been said.

There is, however, practicality in this process, for encouraging a client to

[1] Egan (1975) discusses in more detail the nature of empathy.

elaborate and construct his problem. As the client dries up and seems unable to easily articulate his thoughts (often because he believes the listener would not be interested) he is encouraged to further continue by the listener feeding back the last thing said: "you have been saying that there are a lot of problems with the supervisors . . .". By tailing off in feedback the client will normally warm to his subject once again. It works well because it is common for a person to pause as he continues to think about his subject and then feel embarrassed after the pause; or simply because a pause is commonly used by other people as their opportunity to say something. The consultant controls his desire to make a few 'important' points but rather indicates an interest in further elaboration. This contrasts with the passive role of responding to silence with silence – the client often construes this as disinterest rather than the giving of time and space.

A practice not dissimilar from that described above is commonly used by behavioural science consultants and follows a similar script: "that's very interesting I wonder whether you could say a little more about that". It is less constraining of the client than naming the topic which sometimes tells him too much of the slant you think he should be taking. While this type of intervention is not designed to enable doziness on the part of the listener, nevertheless it is a deliberate strategy which is useful if you should drop off to sleep for a few minutes. It is intended to invite further elaboration (on a topic you do not wish to name) in a 'friendly and positive' way.

INTERVIEWS

So far we have not mentioned the sort of interviewing where the interviewer runs through a list of questions devised in advance. Our reason comes from our wish to emphasize the importance of empathy for the early stages of problem construction, and our belief that structured interviews of a question/answer nature are not good for allowing the client to present the problem 'as he sees it'.[2] This should not be taken as an overriding point of view – there are often circumstances where careful interviews will be successful.

A variation on traditional interview methods is to invite the client to phrase a question to ask himself which will facilitate his telling you aspects of the problem that are particularly significant, but which he would normally only think about rather than articulate. This is particularly helpful when 'illegitimate' political data is important. The sort of question that seems to have worked well in these circumstances goes something like:

> "If you were to fall ill and be away from the office for a couple of months what would you need to tell your temporary replacement about the issue in order that he would act 'sensibly' in your absence? We may assume this

[2] This belief is congruent with most current views on the conduct of interviews in social research.

replacement to be a person you trust and to be as generally and technically competent as yourself – indeed it might even be yourself!''

This type of question usually helps the client 'get at' his thinking about those aspects of the issue which are difficult to articulate and yet are important. Typical content will elaborate the political environment of the client, and the highly subjective judgements which could not be supported by 'hard facts' but nevertheless are a crucial reflection of experience and wisdom.

INTERSUBJECTIVITY

A device which is particularly useful when a problem belongs to a project team is the use of cards for establishing the structure of ideas mentioned by several members of the team.

The process involves the consultant in conducting brief interviews with each team member and trying to record the ideas (constructs) that seem most salient in that person's general description of the problem. From the total list of ideas obtained from all members about forty are chosen so that the cards selected are representative of all contributions. Each idea is written onto a separate card and then all the cards introduced to each member of the team. The team members are then each invited to organize the cards in any way which seems to be appropriate to them. Most people choose to set them out on a table or desk where special distances represent some sort of interconnectivity; some people put them in piles or groups; some people set out their relationship one to another as if they were dominoes; and others go through them talking about the importance and relevance, or not, of each idea.

The point of the exercise lies not so much in what each person has done with the cards but rather with the commentary which usually goes with the organization of the cards.[3] It is this commentary which provides the basis for problem identification from the merging of different perspectives. It is thus possible to gain structure in problem identification without losing individuality – a form of 'intersubjectivity' can emerge.

MORE STRUCTURE

A body of theory known as the Theory of Personal Constructs has been very significant to our way of understanding how people make sense of events.[4]

---

[3] Our experience, so far, has indicated that this technique invariably leads to animated commentary (see Eden and Wheaton, 1980). Our initial feelings, that it would appear to be a silly and pointless game, have not yet been supported by field experience.

[4] Although Kelly originally published two volumes of his theory of personal constructs in 1955, the first three chapters of this work have been published under the title *A Theory of Personality* (1972). These chapters are the most fundamental expression of Kelly's philosophical and psychological views about the nature of man.

Applications of the theory were originally developed for use in psycho-therapy, but they can sometimes be helpful in providing a structure for the client in his attempts to articulate and understand a problem he faces. This comes about because the structured nature of the process helps provide both the problem-owner and -helper with cues and prompts for constructing the problem.

The basis for making sense of our world is taken to lie in our use of experience by seeking similarities and differences. This simple notion led to the practice of introducing to therapy patients three 'elements', selected at random from a list of about twelve elements. Each element is an object (or can be treated as an object) by the patient — thus in most therapeutic circumstances the elements are usually people who are significant in the patient's life. In an organizational setting elements could be different projects, products, market sectors, or elements (problems) of the issue the client is addressing (those elements being jointly identified during initial discussions), and in some instances the elements might be other people such as members of a project team, fellow executives, etc.

Similarity and differentiation is elicited[5] from the client by:

(i) writing the name of each element on a separate card;

(ii) presenting the client with a random selection of three cards;

(iii) asking the client to state "in what way would he regard two of them as similar and yet different from the third?";

(iv) make a note of the descriptive dimension (or 'construct' used to compare the triad of elements. The description of similarity is regarded as one side (or 'pole') of the construct and the description of differentiation as the other pole;

(v) another three elements is randomly selected and the client again asked to compare them. In some cases the client struggles to see any way of comparing the elements — if this is the case then the triad should be ignored and another selected. Often the opposite occurs; the client can elaborate at length on the similarities and differences — here the client should not be constrained (the object is to help elaboration and problem construction) but rather each descriptive dimension used should be noted and an attempt to establish both poles of the construct should be made.

The process should be continued until the client is able to continue problem construction/description without the help of structure; or until about the same number of constructs as elements have been elicited. For example:

The client reports a problem which has been labelled 'inadequacy of information system'. During initial discussions with the client we can identify some possible elements which are related to the problem (see below); how-

---

[5] For a description of how this process, called the Repertory Grid test, was originally devised see Kelly (1955) or Bannister and Fransella (1971).

ever, the client seems unable to articulate his concerns and thus a structured method seems as if it could be helpful.

Possible elements:

1. Current weekly computer printout.
2. Informal knowledge gathered over a drink or lunch.
3. Regular reports from our staff.
4. Current monthly computer printout.
5. Interactive terminal in own office.
6. Interactive terminal in general office.
7. Weekly team meeting.
8. Information services person in department.
9. *Ad hoc* team meetings.

The consultant randomly selects a triad,[6] say,

ad hoc meetings,
current monthly computer printout,
weekly team meetings.

The client's reply was

"information at meetings is relevant to the issue at hand and not full of other extraneous data — most of the printout is irrelevant" (i.e. 9 and 7 have been differentiated from 4).

We would note the constructs as

"relevant to the issue at hand . . . irrelevant to the issue at hand",
"not full . . . full of extraneous data".

Another triad, say, 2, 9 and 7

"weekly meetings are formal whereas the things I get to know at lunch or at *ad hoc* meetings are much more subjective but very useful"

giving the constructs

"formal (data) . . . subjective (data)",
"very useful (data) . . . (not so useful data)".

Here some parts of the constructs (those in parentheses) have been implied by the consultant, and might be checked later if there is time. And so the process continues.

It is possible to continue to a more formal activity by using the elements and constructs to form a grid, and then ask the client to rate numerically the relevance

---

[6] A table of random numbers is useful here, such as the last digit of telephone numbers in a directory. Intuitive random numbers are notoriously non-random.

of each construct to each element. The reasons this might be done are: it may be helpful to explore the clustering and separation of elements and constructs; or, you may be unable to think of any other way to keep open a dialogue with the client.

A grid is completed by asking the client to consider every construct against every element and rate, on any scale, the appropriate way the construct is used, thus:

CONSTRUCTS	relevant – irrelevant			
	!			
	! not extraneous – extraneous			
	! !			
	! ! formal – subjective			
	! ! !			
ELEMENTS	! ! ! very useful – not so useful			
weekly printout	9	7	1	4	etc.
lunch, drink meetings	3	4	9	4	etc.
regular reports	2	2	6	3	etc.
–	–	–	–	–	etc.
–	–	–	–	–	etc.

The client has shown a belief that the weekly printout is mostly irrelevant (rated 9) whereas lunch meetings are fairly relevant (rated 3).

Standard cluster analysis methods can be used[7] to group constructs that are used in a similar way and thus might have a similar meaning, and group elements that seem to have similar attributes. However, the usefulness of a cluster analysis is dubious: its results are often difficult for a client to understand and seem to be hardly worth the fairly laborious undertaking of completing a matrix. Nevertheless, there is no general rule, and experience of using grids with oneself as the 'client' is the only satisfactory way of knowing how to make the judgement about when it is appropriate to use them with a client.

The above example uses data from a project which was designed to investigate the attitude of senior managers of a large company to the provision of decision-making information. After a small number of open-ended interviews the grid was designed and submitted to all the participants. The results of analysis were used as the vehicle for an extremely successful discussion on the effectiveness of the computer-based information system. As a consequence of the analysis and the discussion the information sciences department were able to effect substantial

---

[7] The cluster analysis is manifestly easier if it is undertaken by a computer. There are several packages for understanding the whole of a Repertory Grid process, from triading to analysis. See Jones and Eden (1980) and Armstrong and Eden (1979) for examples of using grid methods in an organizational setting. See Easterby-Smith (1980) for a general summary of grid methodology as it applies to training and organizational development.

changes to the provision of management information. Neither this department nor the managers believe that their attitudes would have been aired without the control and structure given by the grid as the method for eliciting the dimensions of thinking about the usefulness of information.

DISCOVERING GOALS AND OBJECTIVES

A natural extension of grid methods, which can provide a structure for learning more about the reasons why a person is anxious about a problem, is to try and elicit data about what is important to the person[8] as it relates to the problem. The approach may provide insights about the aspects of the situation which are worrying and also preferences about an alternative possible future as it is imagined by the client.

Recent decisions that the client believes he has made relating to the issue under discussion are taken as elements in a triading process for eliciting 'good/ bad' outcomes. The triad question is "in what way did two of these three decisions produce outcomes that are different from the third?"

Having elicited about twelve different constructs, which are descriptive dimensions for outcomes, the client is next invited to answer, for each outcome, the question "why is the outcome you describe either preferred or not preferred?" The answer to this question is generally a further outcome — the question is continuously repeated until the client 'dries up'. Typically each question elicits an outcome which is a more general description and closer to being an 'ideal' preference — that is, an outcome which is desired in an idealistic but not practical sense. In principle the consultant is attempting to identify the idiosyncratic network of goals, objectives and ideals which are relevant to the issue.

As with the use of the repertory grid it is possible to extend this structured problem construction aid and explore the relationship between outcomes by producing an 'implications' grid — that is a grid where both column and row contain the same items, in this case outcomes. The grid is then completed by asking "does outcome 'k' have any implications for the achievement of outcome 'j'?" The replies can be rated, but may include negative ratings in those cases where one outcome is believed to have negative consequences for another. Drawing a diagram of this network of outcomes and feeding it back to the client can be a helpful step in problem construction.[9]

Related to the principle of 'acting stupid' are some common techniques used by social researchers in organizations. The researcher affects 'not to know what

---

[8] A formal basis for distinguishing ideals, objectives and goals can be found in *On Purposeful Systems* (Ackoff and Emery, 1972, pp. 50—57). Their relationship to problem construction is discussed by Eden and Sims (1977).

[9] For a more detailed discussion of this technique and its relationship to ideas about 'value systems' see Eden, Jones and Sims (1979). For an example of its use in a local government setting see Eden (1978).

is going on' and pleads complete naivety about the circumstances of the client. Often this can be achieved by just simply being about the organization – persons will usually approach the researcher in order to try and find out what he is doing, but in the act of inquiry will delight in explaining 'what is really going on round here'. Clearly such techniques can be damaging to the internal consultant who is supposed to know something, but can be effective for the outside consultant/ researcher.

COMMENT

The techniques introduced above are rarely used singly or in totality; their main purpose is often to 'get things going'. After many years of using all these techniques they inevitably have a general impact on the style of interviewing a problem-helper uses in practice. Often the different techniques become an implicit part of the script used to help a problem-owner articulate his problem. We should, however, reiterate our belief that confidence in their applicability and practicability comes mostly from having used them on oneself. In most cases it is possible to gain some view of them without needing to persuade a colleague to try the method out with you at the receiving end – some insights are possible by being consultant to yourself.

Case Study

Jenny wondered whether to take her baby tape recorder with her, but decided it was too early – Alan and John could well feel threatened and so she might find at the end that her interviews consisted more of neat, tidy, insipid and carefully worded statements. She decided that she would be better off simply letting them talk and then putting her own notes on to a pocket dictating machine immediately after the meetings. This would mean that she could devote all her energy to looking interested and encouraging them to talk freely. After John's annoying mistake about what she was going there for she was also determined to make sure she set out her ideas about her possible role at the beginning of each interview. There was at least some advantage in Ian's not having said much to either of them about what she was to do, it meant she had more freedom to interpret her specified task in the way she thought would be most advantageous.

These first meetings could well set the tone for the rest of the project and so she spent a good while pondering on the best style for approaching Alan and John. "If only I'd had a chance to have a natter to Ian over lunch or a drink I'd have a better idea of what tactics to adopt" she mused. However, she was passing Leakey tomorrow and thought it worth dreaming up an excuse for calling and trying to have a 'gossip' with Linda, Ian's secretary.

In the event a chat with Linda proved to be extremely valuable. "Of course Alan's a bit of a boffin – wanders round in tatty clothes and spends half his life on the shop floor getting his new ideas built." "He's here till all hours of the night." "I've been with Ian Brown for several years — he's wonderful — he'll sort Alan out. It's not that he doesn't respect him; he just wishes he'd be more commercial." "John's a nice person. He might have been the marketing director but he's not really aggressive enough", said Linda, proud to be the font of knowledge about the company. "Just the kind of information I needed", thought Jenny.

She now felt a little more prepared when she met John for lunch. Linda was quite right; he did seem to be a nice polite man who was anxious to be helpful. Apparently, after the telephone conversation she had had with him when he was in Alan's office he had gone to check up on her and Linda had said that she was doing something for Ian which needed John's help, so he was treating her with care. She told him that she thought her role was to build a computer model of the market in order that a new product strategy could be developed.

"Why does Ian want a computer model of the current market if he's thinking about new products? Surely he needs a bit of standard market research?" he stated rhetorically. He had put his finger on the niggle that Jenny had. She remained silent hoping John would go on to answer the question. "Anyway, I'm not sure what I can do to help", he added. She decided the best way of progressing was to get John talking about his own product range so that she could get a feel for the market. It is rarely difficult to get someone to talk about his own field. John talked for most of the lunchtime, Jenny needed to provide little encouragement except for playing back a statement of John's every now and again to set him rolling once more. John was thorough, articulate and seemed clear in his own mind about the nature of his customers, the market segment he was satisfying, the size of the market, and what the future held. In one sense she was getting too much hard data given that she didn't have her notebook. John definitely gave the impression that his area was so well planned and straightforward that it was not likely to be of particular interest in Jenny's project, but he "would be very pleased to help in any way — good new products were clearly crucial to the future of the company". They separated at the end of lunch on friendly terms. Jenny felt that he probably would help — in a sort of 'proper' manner, but that he would be surprised if she needed to come back to him.

When she got to Alan's office she found him kneeling on the floor with what appeared to be hundreds of parts to what she presumed must be a new Leakey tap design. His office was chaotic in a sort of orderly way. "Bloody marvellous — this new valve of mine," he said, "can't understand why Ian wants to stop work on it." These were his first words! "Sorry, but it's so bloody ridiculous", he added as explanation.

Alan continued alternately to enthuse about some of his design interests and to grumble about Ian's reluctance to let him go ahead and put them all into practice, as he always had under the previous marketing director. Jenny realized he was not really a client! It was beginning to dawn on her that Alan was being involved in the project 'for his own good'. Whichever way she looked at it she was going to have to try and gain his confidence and gradually persuade him to be a client of her work. She could make this meeting a time to let him tell her about his problems and for her to demonstrate some understanding of them, and maybe even sympathy.

"I know Ian wants me to act as the main link between you and him so that it doesn't tread on the toes of any of the marketing managers, but the trouble is that I am very pressed for time. I hope you can get this model finished as soon as possible so that I can get on with the real work. These ideas I'm working on at the moment are the future of the company." "So that's how Ian explained Alan's involvement in the project", thought Jenny.

Jenny suggested that if the two of them could pool their different skills and knowledge then the project could be completed fairly rapidly – he with his knowledge of the products and the way the company worked and she with her modelling experience. Her current thoughts were that she would produce a model which could explore the prospective contribution each of the current products could make to the future cash flow of the company, a mixture of forecasts at the macro and micro level combined with costs and demand schedules.

"To get things moving could you tell me about what's going on at present around the current product range?" Jenny invited in as open a way as she could think of. Alan accepted the invitation and started talking about where "the real future of the company lies", which in his view was the industrial products division managed by Peter Williams. It turned out that Alan tended to ramble a lot and seemed, to Jenny, to wander on to all sorts of irrelevant topics. He was articulate but difficult to listen to. Jenny was taking extensive notes and found herself particularly interested in some of the topics that kept cropping up. She started to think about how she could best demonstrate her interest in what he was saying; she was nodding a lot and doing all the usual non-verbals but felt she needed to give a good demonstration that she was taking in what he was saying. The trouble was she wasn't sure she could feed back her listening because of the disconnected nature of his commentary. She decided it was time to try 'the cards' as a method of bringing some structured elaboration and getting some more definite interaction between the two of them.

She did not find it difficult to select from her notes some central concepts. He had talked about all of the following:

valves for water flow . . . non-aqueous valves
major breakthrough
bog standard work
using engineering and foundry . . . plastics
making good products better
exciting, challenging work
research on fluid flow
good engineering

where the future lies
totally new market
importance of price
good industrial design
the real purchaser
has to be sold hard
the end user
link with University
the mainstay of the company
developments in materials
luxury products

These were linked to

Ian's old division
John's division
Peter's division
builders merchants
architects
water boards

She scribbled these onto some postcards and said, "You've been extremely helpful in the last hour or so, and given a lot of useful data. I'm afraid I'm not too sure how everything fits together. I've been putting some of the things you seem to think are central on to these cards and I wonder whether you could lay them out on your desk in the way that seems to make some sense to you. If you think there ought to be others that I've missed let's add them in, and if you could explain things as you do it I would find that helpful."

As he looked through the cards he seemed pleased that Jenny had picked up some of the things he thought were important — most people had seemed to miss the significance of some of these things he said.

After he had looked through them once and said a bit about several of them (which enabled Jenny to put on the cards his 'rather thans'), he set about organizing them. "Am I doing this right?", he asked a few times, and Jenny had to work hard to persuade him to do what he liked with them. She began to wish she had after all brought her tape recorder; by now she reckoned it wouldn't have interfered with Alan. Gradually Jenny felt able to join in by asking questions through her moving the cards. Indeed the final displays were two by Alan — one setting out the cards according to how things were now and a second showing a picture of things to come, and one by Jenny which was her attempt at displaying the sorts of things that her model could help him think more about.

Alan seemed pleased by the time she left, and, more important, she felt she had developed a rapport with him that did not leave him feeling she was there to 'do him down'. In her mind the model was beginning to change its form slightly.

She wondered whether it would be more fruitful if she was to construct a series of possible versions of what the company and its product range might look like in the future — these would be static models but with financial and market share predictions. Although Alan was aggressive at the beginning of the meeting she found herself beginning to like him and be wary of his sharp thinking — behind the rambling style was a quick mind.

At the end of the meeting they had agreed to meet again after Jenny had had time to put together a few ideas about where to go next. Even though he seemed more favourably disposed at the end of the meeting she was worried about his frustration over the developments being frozen. This frustration was bound to keep messing up their relationship. She thought that it might be worth thinking of a way of persuading Ian to unfreeze at least one of his projects. Maybe if she talked to Alan about it next time she could do something about this and do it so that she finished up with some credit with Alan.

4

Interactive Modelling

This chapter considers direct interactive modelling as a semi-structured approach to helping a client construct his problem. It is more sophisticated than the approaches discussed in the last chapter, although it has similarities with a structured interview method and uses the model building process as the means for devising 'appropriate' questions. We shall first consider a specific example as a means of introducing the model-building process known as 'cognitive mapping'. In the later part of the chapter we deal specifically with the general topic of the practice of mapping and give some general examples of particular aspects of the mapping process.

PROBLEM CONSTRUCTION USING MAPPING

Cognitive mapping is a modelling technique which intends to portray ideas, beliefs, values and attitudes and their relationship one to another in a form which is amenable to study and analysis. The role of the consultant in the early stages of the relationship is to help his client access 'theories' which have been developed through experience.[1] By modelling in this way we are exploring beneath the surface of words: we consider what a phrase means to that individual – what he intends to convey about his world. We shall see later that the principles implicit in cognitive mapping are not arbitrarily related to pragmatic model building but rather are a practical development of the implications of Personal Construct Theory – a psychological theory about how people construe their world.[2]

Here we shall convey the essence of mapping as it is used for developing constructive dialogue with the client. The first step is straightforward – a piece of paper about A1 size mounted on an easel is used and in the centre a label for the problem is noted. In Chapter 2 we discussed how problems are found in groups and how an agreed label is usually what is noted as the problem. For example,

"production output dropping quickly"

Next ask the client to think about the satisfactory alternative to this circumstance.

[1] Wittgenstein (1953) suggested that "the aspects of things that are more important for us are hidden because of their simplicity and familiarity".
[2] See Kelly (1972).

The client is to be encouraged to think in terms of his own circumstances rather than some 'official' point of view. In one sense the client is being asked to consider what the alternative situation might be which would mean that he was not hassled by the problem, rather than necessarily that which would be regarded as the best situation. For example,

"production output dropping quickly . . . steady output"

It is sometimes difficult for the client to provide an answer to this question; when this is so the consultant may find that the alternative image becomes apparent as the discussion continues. In the example above we may suppose that the official line would have been 'output rising', but personal views indicate 'steady output'. In the second chapter we discussed politics and its importance for how problems are defined. In all organizations there will be good reasons why the client will want to feed you with all sorts of splendid sounding opposites such as 'output improving'. Little will be gained by trying to force a client to admit that he is not psychologically committed to an officially acceptable target. Nevertheless it is also possible that a high trust relationship will allow for a more open admission of the problem as it is seen by the client. Whichever is the circumstance it is still important for the consultant to know how the client sees things, even if the explicit discussion and model displayed to the client and his colleagues contains politically acceptable features.

The next step is to develop ideas through addressing the question "why does this matter to you? Why are you worried about it?" For example, see Figure 4.1.

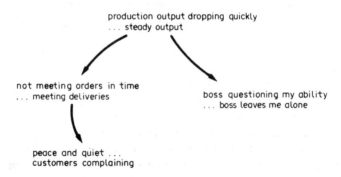

FIG. 4.1.

This is a model which could be constructed in response to an answer: "well, I'm mostly worried about it because it has resulted in the boss questioning my ability, I would feel much happier if he just left me alone. . . . I suppose it's also a problem because we're not meeting orders on time and so it's broken the peace and quiet that exists when customers aren't ringing and complaining about delivery."

Psychological Opposites

In the map developed so far we can see the ideas relating to contrast and similarity being expressed by noting psychological opposites for each concept. The concepts have then been related to one another using arrows to show the belief that one idea influences the other. The significance of opposite poles in indicating meaning was discussed in the previous chapter in the context of repertory grids. The idea is that our constructs develop as we discriminate between aspects of our world in order to understand and manipulate events for our purposes. For example, as someone uses the word 'respect', the way in which they use it, what they contrast with it, provides the meaning in that context. It may be, say,

"respect" rather than "treat with contempt"
"respect" rather than "ignore"
"respect" rather than "dislike"

Each pair of descriptions represent different psychological, rather than logical, opposites and thus different meanings — in the same way as we have just used 'logical' as the opposite of 'psychological' to help you, the reader, better understand our meaning. Similarly, in the example above, we understand differently the construct poles "boss questions my ability" with "boss leaves me alone", and "boss questions my ability" with "boss favours me". In the first case we might begin to see someone who probably wants a quiet life; in the second someone who is ambitious — that is, we are theorizing a connotative link between the clients' "leave me alone . . . favours me" and our construct "quiet life . . . ambition".

Causality

In the model constructed above we have included the client's statements that indicate psychological opposites and we have included the implications of causality by using arrows. However, an obvious extension of the arrow (or directed graph) nomenclature is to include that which we hear about the nature of the causal relationship. Following the usual practice for drawing directed graphs[3] we can assign to each arrow a +ve or −ve sign to show the direction of relationship. Thus if the first pole of one construct leads to the second pole of another construct then we assign a −ve sign to the arrow. If the first pole leads to another first pole then a +ve sign is used. These assignations are best made by considering relationships in pairs, and not by considering a string of beliefs.

These mapping methods are demonstrated further by following the example

[3] See, Harary, Norman and Cartwright (1965) for a detailed discussion on directed graphs; and see Axelrod (1976) for an application of simple directed graphs, or influence diagrams in political science.

of problem construction. After asking for reasons "why the problem matters", and allowing the client time to ramble fully in answer, the next question considers descriptions about how the problem arose. The question is posed: "what reasons come to mind as explanations for ('production output dropping quickly')?" For example, as in Figure 4.2.

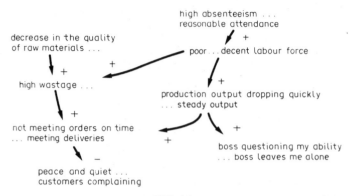

FIG. 4.2.

Once this stage has been reached the problem is beginning to take shape in an explicit model which clients can generally easily understand. They begin to be assured that you, the consultant, are listening to them – for the evidence of your attempts at empathy is before them. The model is not only evidence of careful listening. As we remarked earlier the client will often say 'illegitimate' things using non-verbal forms of communication. He will not want this sort of communication to be reflected in the map but will be anxious for some indication that you have 'heard' what he has said.

Although the content and structure of the model may appear obvious and possibly trivial, it is easily appreciated that the meaning of the problem to this particular individual is becoming more specifically known. Indeed, even though the number of concepts contained in the model is small it is possible to imagine how the meaning of apparently the same problem (one with the same label) for another person in the same organization could be significantly different. The difference can be simply identified using the same approach and comparing model content and structure. So, for example, a model may contain some of the same constructs but differ in the structure of relationships (arrows) which link them – that is their meaning is significantly different. For example, see Figure 4.3. In this sketchy map we can see that there are some similar concepts to those in the map shown below. However, the differences significantly change the meaning of the problem labelled 'production output dropping quickly'.

After the initial discussions have reached the stage given by the above model, and the client has witnessed the model gradually grow, it is likely that each idea on the map leads the client's thinking backwards or forwards to further elaboration of consequences or explanations. For example, see Figure 4.4.

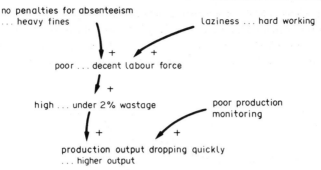

FIG. 4.3.

FIG. 4.4.

If the client seems reticent to expand his description of the problem it is now very easy for the consultant to directly invite the client to consider the "why does it matter?" and "why is it like that?" questions for every concept on the map. In practice the consultant will invite elaboration around those concepts which seem most significant; significant in the sense that encouraging articulation might reveal imaginative explanations and consequences which might be worth considering as a part of a portfolio of possible solutions.

It seems that the opportunity and encouragement to articulate thinking, and see it reflexively in a model which relates ideas as well as noting them, can release anxiety about the issue and open up creative opportunities. The deliberate notice taken of opposite poles of constructs contributes to the possibility of creative thinking. Indeed what is happening here is that the nature of the issue is gradually changing as articulation and modelling take place.

COGNITIVE MAPPING TECHNIQUES

Using the context of mapping as a means of encouraging the client to talk the previous section has introduced the broad principles of mapping. For the remainder of this chapter we shall consider some of the specific issues of mapping. A 'cognitive' map is so called in order to lay emphasis on the idiosyncratic aspects of the model constructed — it is not supposed to be a scientific model of an objective reality in the way some influence diagrams are (for example, those used by System Dynamics modellers[4]), but rather be a representation of a part of the world as a particular person sees it — it can never be shown to be right or wrong, in an 'objective' sense. At all times it is important to consider whether the map is adequately representing the beliefs (implied or explicitly stated) of the client, or yourself. A belief should be clearly attributable and owned by one or other of these two persons rather than its being a muddled version of something the client said and which has then been half-heartedly modified so that it is not owned by either person. Indeed, at the stage of the model we have so far reached the consultant is concerned with modelling so that the beliefs represented are owned by the client.

The Stated or Implied Belief?

The impression is that cognitive maps are totally dependent upon language — they can be, but we believe that such a constraint is damaging to the potential for satisfactory problem construction. During any dialogue each person uses a range of techniques to inform the other; the most obvious of these is the use of language, but there are also other methods of a non-verbal nature. Some of these unintended mannerisms, or rhetoric, or other behaviour are designed to add drama and entertainment; but many will be deliberately meaningful intonations, emphasis by gesture, or emotive overtones. It is sometimes possible for the consultant to find or invent a verbal construct that partly signifies that client's non-verbalized meaning. The consultant should not resist doing so — there is no reason why a cognitive map must be constrained to constructs the client states explicitly, it is more important to portray meaning which is owned by the client. One aspect of mapping mentioned earlier can be useful in the tentative growth

---

[4] Diagrams using arrows in this way appeared in *The Limits to Growth* (Meadows *et al.*, 1972). However, the use of directed graphs to help managers consider important causal relationships has been discussed by Roberts (1976) and Stearns (1976, 1978).

of the model – the connotative link. Consider, for example, the different ways in which a radio writer will attempt to transmit meaning compared with a television writer.

In many interactions the consultant will have with his client the client will be trying to tell the consultant about the 'illegitimate' aspects of the problem. Because such aspects as internal politics of the type discussed in Chapter 2 are illegitimate parts of a problem the client is often unable to state them linguistically; however, the client will still try to sound warnings, grind his own personal axe, and emphasize particular features of the problem by using a battery of non-linguistic methods of communication. This means the client is able to truthfully say "I never said that!" but at the same time influence the consultant. In these circumstances the consultant will be foolish to ignore this type of data and yet will not wish to record it in the model to be displayed to the client but will certainly wish to make it a part of his own model of how the client views the problem. At the same time the client will need some sort of confirmation that the consultant has 'heard' the illegitimate communication. We have referred elsewhere to this transaction as "bluff and double bluff" in the consultant–client relationship.

Connotative Links

Conversation often requires that a series of different phrases are used as if they have the same, or linked, meaning. Alternatively, attributes of a construction are given to help the listener understand more clearly the image the speaker is trying to transmit. A person may say, "a good teacher is excited by his subject and yet is also organized and informal, whereas other teachers just do it for a job and seem chaotic and often severe in their relationship with students."

Within this statement there are no clear causal beliefs, and yet the linking of ideas, constructs, is important for understanding the particular image the person is trying to build of a good teacher. We can usefully depict the elements of the statements by using links between bi-polar constructs, as shown in Figure 4.5.

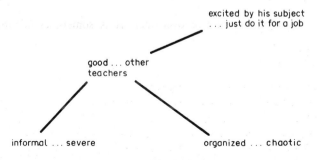

FIG. 4.5.

Maps such as the one in Figure 4.5 can be used both within and outside a normal 'causal' map. They are effective ways of portraying differences in meaning amongst a project group. It is not merely pedantry to explore, and expend energy, identifying the different images persons have of an important element of a problem. For example, if a group of students were acutely dissatisfied with their teaching then we may say they have identified, and own, the same problem. However, before there could ever be a sound basis for concerted effort to change these circumstances there would be a need to explore what each person idiosyncratically means by 'good teaching'. Attribute maps are an effective way of doing this. After negotiation it may be possible for the group to agree about the attributes that are important for construing bad or good teaching. From an aggregated attribute map it may then be helpful to construct a Repertory Grid using different teachers as the elements, and the contents of the attribute map as the constructs in the Grid. Each member of the group can complete the grid so that their teachers can be compared.[5]

It may be helpful to consider the two extreme cases of misunderstanding that can be illustrated using attribute maps (Figure 4.6).

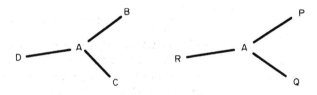

i. same verbal tag (A) used with different meaning

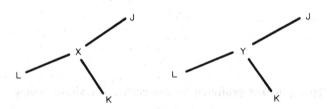

ii. different verbal tag (X and Y) used with the same meaning

FIG. 4.6.

[5] Armstrong and Eden (1979) conducted an exercise along these lines to help a group of estate managers become a more cohesive group. They used a combination of Repertory Grids and Implication Grids to explore differences in meaning (implications grid) and differences in the use of these constructs (rep grid).

Technical Problems in Coding Language

Coding language for maps can often present interesting problems. Is there any significance to the first pole of a construct? Rather than coding an historical explanation as an-explanation, would it be more useful to treat it as a general theory about the future and so code it as a possible consequence? How much of what is said should be included on a map? When a person talks he rarely provides explicit psychological opposites – should they be guessed or left as a void pole?

Every consultant who uses mapping to help problem construction seems to develop his own rules about the significance of the first pole of a construct. The following rules are most common.

(i) The first pole represents the clients description of the current situation, and thus the second pole is taken to be a description of a possible future. For example, "high absenteeism instead of reasonable attendance has been causing chaos with work scheduling ... if only we could set steady work schedules then machine productivity would increase" would be coded as:

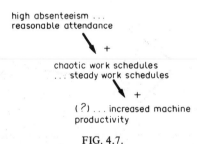

FIG. 4.7.

Generally this method means that the map can be easily read because most arrowheads are +ve signed, and so reading follows down the first poles, or down the second poles.

(ii) A second way of coding makes the first pole represent the descriptive dimension first proffered by the client. The above coding is the same except that "increased machine productivity becomes the first pole and the arrow is thus –ve signed". The advantage of this method is that a glance at the first poles on a map can give an indication of the personality, attitude and general approach of the client to problems. It will often also be an indication of the culture of problem ownership in the organization. Thus, if the first poles are descriptions of the current problematic situation then we may conclude that the issue is construed through a sense of dissatisfaction. If the first poles are predominantly about the 'world as it might be' then we may feel that the issue is construed through a more optimistic vision. It is often helpful to make a note of such differences amongst project team members working on the same issue.

(iii) Another way of coding makes the first pole represent that description which is believed, by the consultant, to be the positive circumstance — that which is regarded as 'best', desirable, or most preferred. In this case the poles are generally referred to as the 'positive' and 'negative' poles rather than first and second poles. The above coding would now be as shown in Figure 4.8 which is, coincidentally, the reverse of the first method. This method seems to be easier because a quick look at the first poles gives an impression of the 'better future'. However, it can be impossible to work when coding the views of a group of people, or the views of a confused individual.

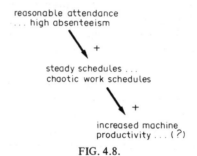

FIG. 4.8.

(iv) There are some who do not believe that it is important to have any rule about the significance of each pole.

The second problem mentioned in Figure 4.8 concerns the relationship between historical explanation and their reinterpretation as prediction. For example, "my policy ideas did not get accepted because I didn't get the advance support of the chairman", can be strictly interpreted as historical explanation, or alternatively can be translated into a future context on the map. The latter approach is generally more helpful, and takes history as the basis for a more general theory with applicability for future planning. A similar problem exists when a person says "we need a new computer because the backlog of processing is too big". Although the statement is in the form of an explanation it could also be treated as the future outcome from a strategy; as in Figure 4.9.

In the second case the direction and sign of the arrow have been reversed. There is no clear-cut rule about which way is best; however, it is sometimes useful to adopt a coding rule which always puts that which is most valued at the head of a chain of arrows. This, of course, implies that a decision can be made about that which is most valued.[6] In the example in Figure 4.9 it is possible to envisage

[6] The conceptual significance of values for an understanding of organizational decision-making is discussed in Chapter 3 of Eden, Jones and Sims (1979).

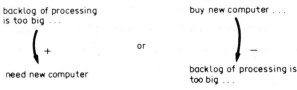

FIG. 4.9.

'buying a new computer' being most valued to the individual (the computer manager?) and reducing backlog to another person; for each of these persons the coding would reflect this difference.

For the consultant it is often important to be aware of these implications even if he chooses not to map in a way which reflects his belief about a client's values. In the Figure 4.9 example it may be unhelpful to the client for a model to represent his personal values in contradistinction to a legitimate organizational goal such as 'reducing backlog'. Nevertheless the consultant would be silly to ignore the personal needs of the computer manager, if he was his client.[7]

How much should be included in a cognitive map? This is a difficult question to answer — it is of the "how long is a piece of string?" variety. It is not usually difficult to make a model large, so large that the client is impressed but loses touch with the central 'features' of his problem. We need to find ways of selecting only those concepts and beliefs that are 'relevant'.

As a person talks about his problem he will make statements which are merely of a 'background' nature and are intended to help the consultant understand terminology. Other than this background data the modeller must attempt to understand the central features of the problem by listening to important values, objectives and goals and then try to ensure that ideas which relate to these values are included on the map. When we discuss later the use of a computer for model building, we shall see how it is possible to consider analytically the relationship between values as they might be identified by the map as a network of 'problems' making an 'issue', and values as we intuitively identified them from our beginning to 'know' our client.

In this way our map is reduced in size by only coding those beliefs which are relevant to areas of interest of the client as if those areas of interest represented a 'problem' arena — something about which the client seemed particularly 'fussed' or anxious, an 'axe he wishes to grind'. There is, however, an acute practical difficulty — how do we do 'on-the-spot' modelling, which requires a rough knowledge of values, when we have not been able to listen long enough to identify values? Our experience suggests that practice seems to make us better at it: that is to say, we have learnt how to use the content of the map as it is being drawn, intonations, non-verbals and other clues so that the mapping accelerates towards a reduction of redundant content. This means that the

---

[7] The distinction between 'personal' and 'organizational' values is discussed in Eden (1974).

early content of a map often turns out to be unimportant and would not appear on a redrawn version.

When should the content of a map be guessed? The third of the questions listed earlier considers when it is appropriate to insert psychological opposites into a map on the many occasions when the client does not provide them linguistically. We discussed earlier the possibility that the early stages of problem construction often results in most concepts being coded as a single pole. We hope we have demonstrated the significance that establishing the opposite pole of a construct has for understanding the meaning of that construct; and therefore asserted the importance of not implying the opposite pole except when it is absolutely obvious. Some concept types seem more amenable to the implication of opposite poles than others, and some dangers exist when an opposite seems obvious but is not.

Some concepts are expressed as if they can be thought of as quantities, whether or not they are measurable. Thus an 'increase in backlog' seems to be of this type. When this occurs it is common practice to ignore the term 'increase' or 'decrease' and code the concept as 'order backlog' where the first pole of such concepts is always taken to be 'increase' and the second pole as 'decrease'. Disadvantages can occur: such coding can upset the coding rules mentioned earlier, e.g. all first poles are taken to be positively evaluated; to imply 'monotonic' concepts can easily miss an opposite pole such as 'no backlog'. When the pole 'no backlog' is set against the pole 'decrease backlog', which may have been presumed, we see that we can miss an importantly different perception of the problem.

In the same way as increase/decrease can be regarded as obvious opposites adjectives such as more/less, up/down, smaller/bigger, etc., can be regarded as obvious opposite poles. This practice can be very dangerous — more so than increase/decrease assumptions. That which is obvious to the consultant would not necessarily have been obvious to the client, but once the consultant has identified the opposite in this way it is unlikely the client will deny it even though it was not in fact the opposite intended. Indeed it is sometimes particularly helpful to 'force' the client to think about alternatives to the 'obvious', apparently logical, opposite pole. By so doing creative alternative circumstances can be defined, and considered as possible solution strategies.

Sometimes statements which seem to have a 'matter-of-fact' sense about them are difficult to imagine as bi-polar. For example, "the world is doomed because the supply of energy is limited" might presume the concept "supply of energy is limited" as a statement of fact and thus of a single pole form. Even though a person might consider that there is no alternative circumstance to "supply of energy is limited" he will be psychologically conceiving an alternative in order for the construct to have meaning. For example, the opposite pole might be "discovery of more sources of energy", which is being negated by the pole "supply of energy is limited". This would be different in meaning to a person who also takes the concept "supply of energy is limited" as a matter of fact but treats it as the psychological negation of "abundant energy".

NEGOTIATING A PROBLEM

The discussion above leads us to consider the stage at which it becomes helpful for the consultant to negotiate with the client and begin to construct a jointly construed problem they both wish to work on. This section discusses the process of negotiation; and the above comments about the extent to which implied meaning can be inserted within the model should be evaluated in the light of strategies for negotiation.

As the client begins to have trust in your concern and respect for his problem then he will become more interested in your appraisal of the situation. The move from an essentially 'empathetic' to a 'negotiative' paradigm can be done self-consciously and effectively by using a model as the vehicle. As we discussed above there are elements of negotiation in the way psychological opposites are, or are not, implied as a map is drawn. A more direct, and positive, approach to problem negotiation comes from a sequence of possible activities undertaken by the consultant:

(i) seeking elaboration in one arena of discussion rather than another;

(ii) broad analysis of a map which suggests to a client the central areas of concern, the concepts which can have most impact on outcomes, the interrelationship of areas of concern or particular problems, the identification of those relationships which if changed would have a significant impact on the nature of the issue, the identification of feedback loops, etc.; and

(iii) the explicit, and acknowledged, act of the consultant constructing his own model of the problem and then merging it with that of the client.

Each of these activities progressively equalizes the power to define the problem and so facilitates an explicit negotiation of the problem which each of the consultant and client see as representing the 'situation' faced by the client.

Any question the consultant chooses to ask will reflect his own interests and view of the problem, thus it is a form of negotiation because it encourages the client to think about one aspect of his problem rather than another. This part of negotiation is clearer when the consultant sees apparently conflictual statements and logical inconsistencies and asks the client to explain these. Consistency and logic are a matter for personal interpretation and concern, thus the act of questioning a client about his problem by implying 'stupidity' can be unhelpful! Nevertheless it is unavoidable for the consultant to direct his line of questioning to an elaboration of conflictual statements. Additionally the consultant may construct hypotheses concerning potential action which are based on the theories already identified within the model: the consultant may say "you've said so-and-so, and so-and-so — if we combine the possible implications of opposite poles would it be true that such-and-such would occur?". A typical answer would be: "no, that wouldn't happen like that because . . ."; and so the model is extended with some of the new content resulting from the consultant's ideas.

Clustering concepts according to the explanations that relate to areas of concern within the issue is one way for the consultant to suggest ways in which each problem relates to another. Key concepts are selected for their appropriateness as descriptions of an area of concern; all concepts which have consequences for this key concept form a group unless they can be included in another group which is subordinate. In this way the relationship between groups can be discovered, and so the inter-relationship of problems noted. For example, see Figure 4.10.

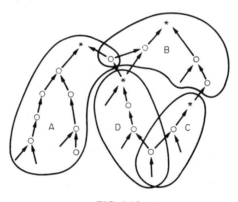

FIG. 4.10.

Figure 4.10 represents a cognitive map, the asterisks are the key concepts, and the shapes which enclose groups of concepts are the interrelating groups. Using the process described above, groups A, B, C and D are established and we discover that they relate to one another as shown in Figure 4.11.

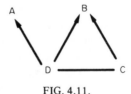

FIG. 4.11.

A and B are superordinate and are not hierarchically linked, D is subordinate to both A and B, whereas C is subordinate to B. If each of these groups of concepts can be identified as areas of concern which make up the issue then we are now able to gain a deeper understanding of the consequences of tackling one or more problems in isolation from others, and also consider the consequences each problem has for others in the context of the complete issue. Grouping concepts in this way provides an interesting basis for negotiation by the consultant and client working from the same map but identifying different key concepts (and thus problem arenas) to work on.

Because a cognitive map is a structure and network it is possible to establish which theories in the map are most sensitive for the definition of the issue. We can see that some theories appear in more sequences of argument from a tail concept to head concept (a tail concept is one with no explanations, and a head concept is one with no consequences). If any of these 'core' theories were changed, or redefined as false, then we can say that the definition of the issue substantially changes. This form of analysis can provide the client with an indication of those theories he might like to question, and conceivably explore their validity by undertaking informal or formal inquiry to determine their 'truthfulness'.

Finally, the most obvious form of problem negotiation occurs when the consultant considers the client's problem from his own point of view. The consultant constructs, for himself, a map representing his own theories about the nature of the problem. After constructing an independent model he can then carefully merge his own map with that of the client so that the new model is a representation of both their views, including conflictual and contrary views. The client is invited to explore both the consultant's model and the merged model. As the exploration unfolds both parties join a discussion which is structured by the merged map, and thus allows the map to change into a negotiated problem definition which often leads to the development of possible courses of action.

Vicious Circles and Stability — Cognitive Feedback Loops

When a client talks about the way the world works he often refers to 'vicious circles' and regards them as things of importance. Vicious circles can be crucial to developing policy; for they can act to support our intentions or alternatively act in a degenerative manner. Once we define ourselves as caught up in them it is usually extremely difficult to break them or change their direction. When we listen to a group of people describe the situation they see as problematic we often find that some of the theories they use join together to produce a loop. A map of these theories shows that a change at any point leads back to itself. For example, in periodical publishing there are some loops which often recur as persons describe the growth or decline of their market. The following theories are utilized at different times to talk about particular aspects of publishing: "more circulation leads to the publication being more attractive to advertisers . . . the bigger the book then the more readers like it . . . because we have to keep a constant ad—ed ratio the more pages of advertising we get the more editorial we produce . . . if the book feels better to the reader, he is more likely to buy it."

If we add to these theories about market behaviour some of the simple arithmetic relationships that exist between the ideas then we have a map which looks like that shown in Figure 4.12.

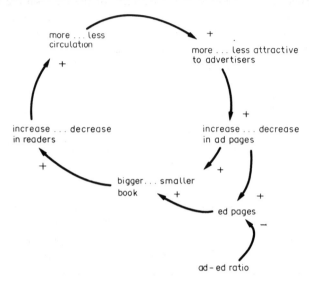

FIG. 4.12.

This represents only one of the possible vicious circles that are often believed to exist for some periodicals. We can see how if we start at any point in the circle and consider possible intervention then the consequences generate growth or decline circumstances; thus if we considered increasing the ad rate in order to intervene on the 'attractiveness to advertisers' then: a decrease in ad pages may lead to a decrease in ed pages (because +ve arrow and the effect of ad—ed ratio) which may lead to a smaller book, which may lead to less circulation, which may lead to less attractive to advertisers, which may lead to a decrease in ad pages, and so on round the loop again, ALL OTHER THINGS BEING EQUAL.

The loop identified is a positive feedback loop. Obviously the same loop could produce growth (all other things being equal) by, say, increasing the attractiveness of the book to the reader with free gifts. Note that all that is needed is a once-and-for-all change of one factor in either direction. It is also important to note that this loop can easily be broken by ignoring the constant ad—ed rule; and it is such discoveries which can be significant to the client, and which he would not have properly appreciated without the use of a model.

Taking one loop in an isolated manner like this reveals a part of the basic behaviour of a periodical market which the client believes persists. However, seeing a model usually encourages the client to identify other theories which interact with those in the loop. Indeed one of the valuable outcomes of mapping is the invitation the model makes to the client to say "it's not as simple as that because . . ."; and so elucidate more of the problem.

Often we find that loops which appear in maps are not vicious but stabilizing. We see in Figure 4.13 a loop of this sort, many of the ideas on the map being similar to those in the vicious-circle diagram.

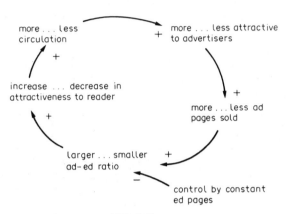

FIG. 4.13.

Following this set of theories we have: less attractiveness to advertiser may lead to less pages of ad sold, which may lead to smaller ad—ed ratio (because ed pages remain constant), which may lead to an increase in attractiveness to reader, which may lead to more circulation, which may lead to more attractive to advertiser; thus stabilizing the initial intervention. With these set of theories and all other things being equal, it would be possible for higher ad rates to result finally in about the same number of ad pages!

Here the circle of ideas forms a negative feedback loop. In this loop we can see how, using the control of constant ed pages, the journal team have created an interaction with the market which aims to maintain the *status quo* as long as there are no other interfering changes. A controlling loop illustrates how theories lead to 'stability'; a budgetary control system is intended to have the same impact where budget variance is the signal for homing back 'on course'.

Diagrams similar to those appearing above are seen as 'influence diagrams' in books on System Dynamics[8] for the quantitative simulation modelling of 'real' systems. As they appear in cognitive maps they are taken to be representations of interpretations of a problem by an individual or group — they represent the 'reality' of that individual or group. We shall discuss later how an 'owned' rather than objective reality model of a problem can be used as the basis for quantitative

[8] System Dynamics was developed by Forrester (1961) and used to construct the well-known world model — Meadows *et al.* (1972). A recent text discussing its use in management is Coyle (1977).

modelling and how the existence of loops within a cognitive map would suggest the use of System Dynamics as a modelling methodology.

Case Study

During the next couple of weeks Jenny started putting together a crude model using some of the data she could easily lay her hands on. Her intention was to produce a small-scale computer simulation model that simply enabled a user to experiment with different market size figures, a variety of cost bases, and a variety of production mixes. She had been working pretty much full time on the project, slaving over a hot terminal, and also getting some rough-and-ready data from John, Peter and Justin (Ian's old deputy in the up-market division — and desperately hoping for Ian's old job). She had also been to see Alan on two further occasions.

Although the exercise with the cards had been about trying to help her sort out Alan's statements by enabling him to provide a structured elaboration, she realized when she got back to her office that she could build a 'first shot' cognitive map of the things she had heard. She did this mostly for her own benefit — she hoped it would give her a framework for understanding Alan, and thus for managing her relationship with him more effectively. The content of the map was mostly implied through her attempt at understanding his view of her and the project. It was not the sort of map to feed back to Alan, or indeed to let anyone see other than possibly her boss!

On the occasions when she had seen John, Peter, Justin and Alan during these two weeks she thought she might get some better insights into the market if she started mapping the content of the interviews. The activity was informal and the maps were not shown to the other people; she concentrated on making sure they saw her as doing some non-threatening data collection. However, she was used to taking notes using maps, and thought it might have some future benefits in helping her decide what direction she should develop her model after the current crude model had been finished.

Her map of Alan's views expanded, even though he usually repeated himself at each of the meetings. His repetition was not because he forgot what he had said last time, but rather to emphasize his arguments so that he could feel more certain that Jenny had fully heard the significance of what he had said. As she got closer to having a working model to show Alan and, she hoped, Ian, she became a little concerned that Alan would not be paying a great deal of attention to the model but would instead be telling her the same things over again. She wondered whether it would help if she had one more meeting with him before displaying the computer model, and used this meeting to feed back some of the beliefs that came out at the last meeting. Maybe if she fed back a map he would begin to realize more fully that she did listen to what he said.

At the last meeting she had drawn the map illustrated in Figure 4.14. It was

FIG. 4.14. An initial attempt at a model following the first interview with Alan.

untidy in the way they usually are when they are taken down as the person speaks; she thought it was worth tidying and drawing out on to an A3 sheet of paper. Most of the concepts on the map had cropped up on previous occasions. The exception to this was the part of the map that directly referred to the reasons why his 'best man is leaving'. She wondered whether she should take out the comments specifically about Alan, but eventually decided that they might demonstrate her interest in his position relative to Ian. She also thought it likely that she could encourage Alan to use the map to think about other explanations and consequences of his beliefs about Ian – how certain was he about his beliefs? What might he do to change the impact of these beliefs? She could think of a few possibilities for redefining the way Ian might see Alan's section. Overall the idea of feeding back the map seemed likely to move Alan towards being a client rather than an unwilling participant in the project.

At the back of her mind she could see that she was going to have to get John, Peter, Alan and possibly Justin together to debate the numbers her model would produce. Inevitably the debate was going to involve all of the ideas that they each had mentioned, ideas that she couldn't possibly get into her model. If each of them found maps interesting then perhaps she could use a structured mapping approach alongside her model as a means of managing the process of discussing future product development. In particular, if she could get Alan interested in the idea of a structured discussion he might feel happier about involving the marketing managers in the project directly, whereas otherwise he seemed to find discussions about new products a waste of time; "It never seems to end up getting anywhere", he had said. Jenny felt that if she were not careful he would accept the involvement of the marketing managers only in the modest role of number suppliers.

So it was that Jenny met Alan two days after her last meeting with him (she liked to get back to people as quickly as possible, before they had lost the impetus of the previous discussion). "At our last meeting you came up with quite a few ideas about where the future lay. It struck me that it might be helpful if I clarified some of these points. What I have done is to put these ideas together into a sort of model so that we can get some more overall feel as to how the ideas relate to one another. I have tried to get it down into a model without distorting what you said. . . . I have split the model in two parts even though you see them as related – the first part seemed to be a group of ideas that relate specifically to 'innovation' and the second is more related to the need to move quickly on the development front." She showed the first (and possibly less sensitive) part to Alan and explained; "What the model is trying to do is to capture some of the explanations and consequences of each idea for others. The arrows simply mean that I thought you saw an idea influencing another. So, for example, I think you said that by the use of new alloys the current products could be up-dated whereas a move into plastics would lose the benefit of foundry skills." Alan remained silent for several minutes – so long that she worried that he might be wondering 'what the hell is it all about?' "You know that's just what I do think about it . . . but it's a bit simplistic like that", said Alan. "Where do you think it's simplistic?", invited Jenny. "Well, as your diagram shows, the core of it all is technological innovation. We can get a really good reputation for advanced thinking — 'the people to come to to solve today's problems', rather than just going from crisis to crisis desperately trying to keep up with everyone else. That way we can charge almost anything we like for our products." He paused, rubbed his chin, and went on; "The current developments in material sciences are not just giving new alloys but also making the cost of plastics prohibitive compared to the use of non-oil based materials, and this means we can make hugely better products for the same price as the current ones."

Alan carried on picking up points on the map and expanding his views about them. As Jenny added these to the map he became more and more fascinated with how ideas seem to cluster. At one point he said, "Look, every time we have a meeting on this area we forget how integrally related all the others are to this one." Jenny noted the labels he used for each area and drew a map of the relating areas for Alan to consider. She also pointed out the possible significance of the loop which meant that higher volume would facilitate the use of new foundry techniques which could lead to more possibilities for updating products.

It was some time before she had a chance to introduce the second part of the map. Alan was, by now, losing energy and didn't want to consider a new topic — he was still quite wrapped up in the first part of the map. She decided to postpone any thinking about Ian's attitude to product development.

She left Alan's office without the map — he wanted to keep it to ponder over. This was both annoying and rewarding. She wanted the record but also was pleased that Alan had been encouraged to work on it further. She promised to call by the next day to borrow and take a photocopy — for a moment this worried Alan, he didn't want anyone else to see it, but Jenny reassured him that it was for her own eyes only.

Her next few days were filled with making minor modifications to her model so that she could demonstrate to Alan how her model contributed to considering the issues that were most important in his thinking.

5

Problems in Teams

We have talked so far mostly about problems that emerge from an individual client, but there are also times when a helper is called upon to work with a team of clients. This may be because no one individual feels he has the knowledge to put himself forward as the person who tells the helper about the problem, or it may be because no one person in the team is trusted by the others to do a good job of describing it. More frequently, however, it seems to be because several members of a team share a feeling that there is a problem, something which they would prefer to be a bit different from the way it is. This does not mean that they can articulate it enough for it to be summarized to a helper. They do not feel that they know what the problem they want to work on is. They do not necessarily think they could all agree on a problem. They probably think that it is complicated enough to need all or at least several of the members of the team to be able to talk about it and give its context together. For these or many other reasons, the helper ends up talking to a team of people. The helper does not usually get to know which of these reasons, or what other reason, lay behind the members of the team taking an interest in that problem, and asking for help in doing so.

We have often found that teams get more from looking at problems together as a team effort than they do from any individual help. For this reason we quite often suggest to our clients that, even if they have brought a problem to us individually, they might prefer that we have a look at it with them and the other members of their team together. The response that we have had to this suggestion, and the effectiveness that has ensued when it has been carried out, leads us to think that this is a form of help which might frequently be taken up enthusiastically by clients if it were more widely offered.

At present, members of a team tend to think of their problems and their teams in a way which is not conducive to thinking of the former in terms of the latter. Many forms of help that are offered purport to start by pin-pointing the 'real' problem.[1] If an expert can come in from outside and tell people what their problem really is, there may not be all that much benefit in talking with the whole team about how they see the situation, rather than just talking with one

---

[1] See Slee Smith (1971, p. 102) for some examples of 'real problem' type statements made by helpers, and which Slee Smith advocates.

or two members. However, the perspective which we outline in Chapters 1 and 2 suggests that you might get quite different views and conceptions about a question by talking with several members of a team rather than with only one, and the view you end up with might be more robust in attempting to solve a problem in that team than would a view culled only from the person who first happened to talk to the helper.

At the same time, there may be some cynicism to be overcome as to whether anything good can ever come out of working in a team. The arguments for and against working in teams need not concern us here;[2] because of the different perspectives, concerns and interests that different members of an organization have, we would expect working in a team to be frustrating (and plenty of team members are willing to confirm that for us) but fruitful. The strength, frustration and indispensability of teams stem from one of the facts of present-day organizational life, that people share power but have conflicting interests.[3]

There are two fields of endeavour that should be able to make a contribution to the understanding of problems in teams, and we have been concerned to bring these skills together as a way of producing the most practical interventions in teams. In the recent past (although many of the elder statesmen tell us that it was not always so, and a rereading of some of the early texts confirms their claim), operational researchers and management scientists have tended to concentrate most on developing their model building skills, and to concern themselves less with trying to improve the way they go about collecting the data that they model. This has resulted in their working mostly with simpler, more quantifiable, cleaner sorts of data — the very last kind of thing that you can expect to get out of talking with most client teams about problems that they care about.

At the same time, using a different body of expertise derived from the applied behavioural sciences, there are 'Organization Development' consultants[4] who have spent a lot of time working with teams, handling mucky data, looking at illegitimate issues (though they too have tended to shy off the organizational politics); in general they have been much broader and more sensitive to uncertainty and confusion in their data collection for their clients. Unfortunately, however, at least by the standards of explicitness and consciousness that are employed by operational researchers, they do not seem to have had very much in the way of ideas about how to lay out and represent back to their clients the data that they collect. Clearly in the case of successful organization development consultants they are doing something helpful and useful with their data, but in most cases this is done at too intuitive a level for others to be able to

---

[2] The arguments against using teams are well rehearsed and popular; "a camel is a horse designed by a committee". For some arguments in defence of teams see Galbraith (1974).

[3] Allison (1971).

[4] For a good introduction to this field see Bennis (1969). For a more recent account of what happens in this style of consultancy, see McLean, Sims, Mangham and Tuffield (1982).

learn the secret of their success, or indeed for the successful consultants them-selves to build as much on their success as they might otherwise do.

Over the last few years we have been adapting the methods that we have talked about in previous chapters for use in teams. We find that they help us to do more than we could otherwise do towards getting the best of both worlds. They give us the explicit models to manipulate and work with that are a great strength of operational research. They also enable us to collect and use the sensitive and more varied data about whatever it is that is concerning the client, which has been more the province of organization development.

In the remainder of this chapter, we shall look first at some of the things involved in managing the social dynamics of modelling problems in teams. After that we will look at some of the difficulties that arise in aggregating different perspectives in a team about a problem, and consider why this is a difficult thing to do. Finally we shall turn to consider the management of ideas and problems in project teams.

THE SOCIAL DYNAMICS OF MODELLING PROBLEMS IN TEAMS

Any helper working with a team has a choice which can continuously be made and remade about how much to dismantle or disrupt the normal social dynamics that pertain in that team.[5] The more the helper intervenes in these dynamics, by causing people to stop and consider what they are doing in their dealings with other members of the team, by pointing out where people are being ignored, and so on, the less likely it is that powerful members of the team will feel that the team is achieving anything during that session, even if they are in principle all in favour of an intervention; however, a skilled helper may be able to make quite major interventions without losing the support of powerful members. At the same time, by intervening in the normal and unconsidered processes of the team, the helper brings the team to see other possibilities of ways they might go about doing their business; if the helper is successful in doing this, and the team discovers from it some different process which they then go on to practise and institutionalize, then an important and lasting contribution has been made.

Even if the helper does not manage anything as grandiose as that, it can be very valuable in problem definition for a team to have a helper present. By being there, asking questions which are probably out of the ordinary for most of the team members, and making suggestions of how they can go about their discussion, they are likely to achieve three things. Firstly, they are likely to enable members to think of points which they would not otherwise have thought of (in this respect, acting as a device for increasing creativity and lateral thinking). Secondly,

---

[5] The concept of disengagement (Mangham, 1977) is quite helpful about this; to what extent does the helper wish to disengage his clients from their world-taken-for-granted?

they are likely to hear points which other members make which would not usually be heard or taken seriously (in this respect, acting as a device for improving listening). Thirdly, they are likely to enable people to say things which they might otherwise have thought of but not said (in this way acting as a more general 'permit to speak'). The reader should remember that the 'helper' we are referring to is not necessarily an outsider to the team. Sometimes a chairman in a team may be particularly well placed to undertake these tasks, although the occupant of that role will often be too enmeshed in the content of the problem to be able to undertake them properly.

We expect, when working with a team, to find a lot of different and even conflicting concepts from the different team members, but also quite a lot of common concepts, or concepts that are similar enough that we can put the maps together in some sort of an aggregation. Very often the team members have all spoken to us separately, and so there is less risk of 'perceptual set' than if we had talked to them all together; by this we mean that there is more likelihood that what each person says to us about the problem does not constrain or influence what the next person says about it. This means that we collect together what often turns out to be a very large amount of separate and partially conflicting wisdom from different members of the team. When they see it all put together, it can be a revelation to them as it explains some of the funny things that have been happening in their discussions about this sort of issue, sometimes for years. The aggregated map can then be presented to the team; if, as is usual, it is by this time a fairly large map (perhaps a couple of hundred concepts or more) the presentation needs to be a careful, deliberate and lively process. There is so much content, there are so many new ideas, so many new possibilities opening up, and new relationships between problems and sub-problems appearing, that if people are not highly stimulated and excited by the presentation, they will probably be swamped by it. Indeed helpers also risk being swamped, unless they have made use of something which helps them to organize the concepts of the map, such as the grouping procedure described in Chapter 4 or the computer assistance described in the Appendix.

Sometimes it is expedient to meet the team all together rather than to begin work with the individual members separately. Building a model in this way can often be more exciting for the team than individual model-building sessions. However, it is much harder with this process to enable points of view to emerge which are of no interest to, or which are actually disagreed with by, the powerful members of the team. However much those powerful figures may intend to be open and receptive to others' views, there will still be those to whom they are accustomed to not listening, and those points which they may have dismissed for some long forgotten historical reason. In some cases one of the skills by which they gained, hold and retain power in their team is the ability effectively to write off some particular people or points in a discussion. When helpers do build their models away from the clients, they may choose to present some of the less-valued contributions in such a way that the power-holders are more inclined to take note of them. This is quite separate from any considerations of whether power should or should not be equalized; it is done in the interests of increasing creativity. It may also be done in order to equalize power if the helpers' values lead them to want to do that. Whether or not they set out to do so, helpers are inevitably intervening in the power relationships in the team. Their mapping, and the selections they make in what they map and how, are bound to have some influence over the power of different contributors.

It is not only in matters of power, but in other factors which are involved in selective perception, that helpers may want to assist in making listening less selective among members of a team than it would have been in their absence. For one thing, including a concept on a map changes it in a way that seems to make people more willing to build on it than to reject it. Also, one of the great incentives to rejecting other people's thoughts is diminished, and that is the threat of finding oneself with a paralysing number of different things to think about – a swamping complexity. It is our experience that when our clients are less anxious about forgetting something vital, or losing their train of thought, they are less dismissive and selective of each others' ideas than they have previously been.

Another thing that often happens when ideas from team members are coded to become part of a map is that members do not just accept each others' ideas – they claim ownership of them. Frequently, we have found that a concept which came from only one member of a team is believed by several (sometimes all) members to be something that they said. In some cases, clients have told us that one or more concepts on the map show great insight on our part, because that was what they meant, but they had never found a way of saying it. When we tell them that this concept came from one of their colleagues, they sometimes do not believe us. Whether or not they believe us, and whether or not this affects their attitude to that colleague, it usually assists their thinking and their contribution to their team.

One thing we have noticed with starting the process of modelling a problem in a team is that quite often, if the modelling is done with the team all together, some of the individuals present may wish to take the jointly produced model away and elaborate it for themselves. In some of our recent work we have encouraged teams to do this, and then we have gone round talking to the individuals about what kind of elaborations they have made of their models, with a view to bringing these elaborations back and putting them together in the team. Where this is possible it seems to be a very good working compromise between the two different approaches to initial mapping that we have described.

AGGREGATING PERSPECTIVES ON A PROBLEM

However the helper goes about managing the social dynamics of modelling problems in teams, at some point there will be a need to put together the views of different persons about problems. Now as we said in Chapter 3, the definitions that individuals have of problems, the views they take of them, are a very idiosyncratic matter. One person's serious problem is another person's intriguing puzzle, and to another person it is not noticeable at all. So how can we go about aggregating these different perspectives?

We all see the world in different ways. There is so much around us that we cannot possibly see everything. Our perceptions and non-perceptions are quite selective. Whilst we could multiply examples of differences in perception, it is worth noting that if we really thought perceptions were totally idiosyncratic, we would not have any reason for talking about them. We assume that there is enough agreement about the meaning of words and the nature of objects that we can, most of the time, reckon that we know what each other are talking about. "Regardless of the philosophical bases of the following two positions, we find the notion that individuals are separate and alone, each inhabiting their own subjective reality, to be, in its extreme form, almost as unhelpful as the opposing notion that the world is a place of facts which can be proved or disproved, and about which we can all be expected to agree."[6] Instead it seems more helpful to take what we call an 'intersubjective' position; what we know about and perceive is basically a subjective matter, but for most of us most of the time there is a great deal of agreement about this knowledge and these perceptions; there is a large area of intersubjectivity, which to all intents and purposes behaves like an objective world.

This begins to give a rationale for producing an aggregated model of a problem. Different people see problems in organizations in different terms, and indeed they are paid to do so. Nobody (apart from, possibly, the personnel officer) wants the accountant to start seeing everything in the same way as the personnel officer; someone has to watch the accounts. Different people see problems in different terms, but to do anything about those problems, they will usually need to act in concert with other independent individuals, and will therefore need to take some account of how those individuals see the initial problem. Thus although it may often be too abstruse for them to think about it in these terms explicitly, many people in organizations find that the way their colleagues see a particular problem is a part of the way they see the problem, even if they disagree with, or disregard, some of the particular points made. So it often happens that members of a team will accept an aggregated model of a problem as being, for each one of them individually, a model which they are more happy to own and to think about than they were with just their own model, however far they had developed that. Models, after all, are not meant to take over the business of thinking, but only to serve as an explicit, manipulable and usable

---

[6] This quotation is from Eden, Jones, Sims and Smithin (1981), where this topic is dealt with more fully.

tool. These tools should assist with thinking about matters so complicated that it is difficult to think about them unaided, and should also act as an aid to communication between the team members about such complicated matters.

In the next chapter we shall consider some of the more detailed practical questions that arise in trying to build intersubjective models to help teams in the consideration of problems.

Case Study

Jenny was glad that things were going so well with Alan. She had got to like him during their sessions together, and was beginning to find his enthusiasm for potential developments in the technology of taps and stopcocks quite infectious.

But she was also getting a little bit uncomfortable. Her original client had been Ian, not Alan, and she felt she should make sure that she was not being seduced into changing product and client unless there was some very good reason for it. Was there such a reason? — she asked herself. On the whole not — but it is very difficult if you are empathizing with a person in a client organization, and listening carefully to what they say, not to get to see things so much through their eyes that you feel that theirs must be the only valid way to look at what is going on.

Jenny decided to talk this through with her boss, because something she did not want was to end up with a project that she was pleased with, but that did not satisfy his interests and his strategic objectives. She was not particularly looking to her boss for advice or directives, but then he had been around in the consultancy and advice-giving business for long enough that she could be pretty confident he would not give her either of those. What she wanted was someone to listen to what she had to say about the project on her behalf, because she could not listen while she was talking!

"The trouble is", she said, "that it looks to me as if Alan might well be right. But Ian's got us there to produce some facts and figures to demonstrate to Alan that he's wrong, at least partly. Now even if he were wrong, and I suppose I'm not qualified to judge that, I don't think there's any way that Alan would or could accept himself as having been proved wrong by this rather oblique new product exercise. So what Ian's got us doing may well be a step in the wrong direction, but in any case, I can't see that it would be likely to work."

Jenny's boss, Arthur Morris, was a reflective man who always liked to pause to think about things before responding. "So you think", he said, "we've got several different perspectives here without the people who've got the different perspectives realizing it?" "That's right", said Jenny, "and all the perspectives are well enough organized and argued in themselves that nobody is going just to abandon theirs. I think if I'm going to do anything there that is of any use to them — including being any use to Ian — then I've probably got to do an exercise with the team as client, so that some of their idiosyncrasies get a bit of an airing and sharing. It could be a bit tricky, because I'm not sure that they're much predisposed to accept one another's peculiarities at the moment. But at least I've got a start, because I've got a well-developed map of Alan, and rough maps for Ian, Justin, Peter and John. The trouble is, that is not what they asked for."

Arthur knew this dilemma only too well; a consultant knows something which they think will help their client, but a client may not ask for what the consultant thinks will do them good, either because some possibility has occurred to the consultant that has not occurred to the client, or because the client knows something the consultant doesn't – often about either the politics of the situation or about their own values.

Arthur also knew that Jenny would be thinking along similar lines to this. She was. "Perhaps what I'd better do", she said, "is to go and put it to Ian that as well as the modelling project that he asked for, I would like to do something that surfaces some of the different ideas that may be around on new products, and existing ones, in a way that is a bit less constricting, and gives rather more freedom for some of the ideas that people aren't quite sure about than does our market modelling. He's a big boy – I don't think he'll have any trouble saying no if he doesn't want to do that."

"Make sure that he knows it's only an optional extra, won't you?", said Arthur.

Now Jenny wanted an appointment with Ian to talk this over with him, and to try and sell him on the way she wanted to go about it. Although she wanted to make the appointment as soon as possible, if possible she would prefer to avoid getting into conversation with him until she had had a chance to think out how to put the idea to him that there were different ideas and approaches within his team, without her actually giving away any confidences. If she did give anything away, she could be quite sure that would be the last she would hear about what they were all thinking.

She rang Ian's secretary. "I'm afraid he's not here at the moment", said Linda. "Oh, never mind", said Jenny, hoping the relief did not show in her voice, "but has he got any free time next week?" "No, he's off to Switzerland with Justin all next week, looking at Sultans' bathrooms", said Linda, "but I tell you what, he's going up to head office this afternoon, and I think he'll have a bit of time. Shall I get him to drop in on you?" "Oh yes, that would be great. I'll be in all afternoon."

Jenny did not actually think it would be all that great. She was trying to finish off a report on some work she had done in Septic Tanks, and she would not have as much time as she would like to think out how to sell Ian on the change of emphasis. But still, she felt that some of the data she had been getting was important, and she did not want the project going cold on her. She had found that clients do not much like to give important data and then to have it dragged up ages after they had given it. She quickly looked at the doodled map she had done of what Ian had said to her; it reminded her of what he was like and what he was concerned about. She did not think he was likely to be too difficult, because he seemed to be quite interested in new ways of looking at things; it should be all right to play it by ear. She then immersed herself in Septic Tanks.

When Ian turned up he seemed more relaxed than he did in his own office. He admired her office, told her where he was going in Switzerland; "Perhaps in a few years, if we get our new product direction sorted out", he said, "they will be coming over here to see what they can import from us, and I'll have to look for a new excuse to go swanning off abroad! Now, what did you want me for?"

Jenny started off by giving him a quick run-down on where she was with the market modelling project. It was going according to schedule, and he seemed very pleased, if a bit surprised, by this. "But I've been thinking", she said, "that there seem to be a lot of people around with different ideas, but nobody knows how, or if, these ideas fit together."

"Hmm", said Ian, "that's my job, isn't it?" Jenny wondered if she had just blown the project, although he did not look offended. "Well, not necessarily", she said. "You quite often find a lot of ideas, when you go round like I have been doing, which everyone assumes everyone else has thought of, but in fact no one else has. That is the kind of thing I think would be worth looking at next with the marketing managers plus Justin and Alan. I think it might help people to be more sensitive to the overall picture", she said, vaguely. This ambiguous sentence was taken by Ian to mean that there were some signs of Alan falling into line. He did not check whether this was what she meant (it was not), because he reckoned that she and he would have both thought that rather improper. "Yes, that sounds useful", he said. "I would be grateful if you would carry on with that line. Are you getting all the access you need?" Jenny realized she had been misunderstood, but could see no way of correcting the impression, and perhaps it did not matter too much anyway if Ian believed what he wanted to believe. Soon afterwards, he went on to the meeting he had come up for; they were both reasonably content with their chat.

6

Model Building in Teams

Clearly, when working with a team rather than an individual client, the problem-helper is dealing with significantly greater complexities. He has to cope with the social dynamics which occur among a group of individuals with different personalities, styles of interaction, power, 'internal' political concerns with respect to one another, beliefs about others' competence levels, and so on. He has also to try and understand the several different ways in which the members of the team give meaning to any overall 'problem label', and a variety of beliefs and expectations about the team/helper relationship. The problem helper will need to be aware of these social dynamics, evolve strategies and tactics for handling them. To build a model which the team members find convincing and useful he will need to facilitate a process by which a team can come to negotiate about a problem definition which they can work on together. This chapter raises some of what we have found to be the more important practical issues surrounding the use of the techniques in this book when working with teams.

ESTABLISHING EXPECTATIONS

The procedures that we have found to work best may start in one of two ways, either with the team members individually talking to the helper about the problem as they see it, or alternatively with a meeting of the team run by the helper for the purpose of their telling the helper about the problem, and at the same time making their ideas open to their team colleagues. What typically happens is that one or more members of the team approach the helper and ask for his help. Arrangements may then be made to meet the rest of the team together so that everybody knows that a consultant is going to come round and talk to them, and knows the rules that will be followed in this procedure. For example, issues of the confidentiality of what is said to him need to be raised at this juncture, as do expectations about how much time he will require, where the meetings should be held, whether they will be tape-recorded or noted in some other way, what 'problem label' will be used as a starting point, how much freedom the members of the client team have to depart from that central point in discussion, and perhaps most important of all, what sort of model the consultant intends to present back to the team of the data that emerges. This last point is crucial for team members who are unsure about how much they can afford to reveal. Whether or not such a team meeting is held, these are critical issues which need to be taken seriously by the helper, and which will need to be discussed widely within the team.

INDIVIDUALS OR GROUPS

There are distinct advantages to initial individual meetings. One simple yet extremely important advantage is that spending time with individuals first of all reinforces the problem-helper's position as wishing to take into account and work with the views of every member of the team. Most importantly, even taking into account that the individual will be selective about what he is prepared to reveal, the problem-helper will learn far more about that particular person's personality, beliefs, concerns and interests in the situation than can be learned when talking to a group. This is not simply a matter of 'air time'. However well the problem-helper manages to ensure that each person has his say, it is impossible to avoid some kind of mental set acting as a boundary to the discussions that occur in a group, with thoughts being channelled by the ideas that have already been expressed by their colleagues.

If the problem is seen by the group members as complicated we find that initial interviews much less than an hour long tend to be rather limited. Shyer or more nervous clients can sometimes take quite a while to settle down and start talking freely, although they may be quite capable of filling up the meantime with platitudes and whatever statements are the equivalent in their organization of speaking in favour of motherhood and apple pie. If the interview is longer than one and a half hours, we find that the attention of both client and consultant tends to flag, however interesting the issue, and however good the interview. So we would usually spend an hour to an hour and a half with each person in the team. Either as they are talking, or subsequently from a tape-recording (often both), we make notes in the form of a cognitive map, in the way we have described in Chapter 4. If we know the client reasonably well, and both he and we are relaxed, we make those notes in a form that he can see and respond to immediately. Sometimes we would take those notes away, tidy them up, and go back to see the client with them in their cleaner form, as soon afterwards as practically possible. Sometimes, for example, it seems important to get back within 24 hours. The longer you leave it, the harder work it is for the client to climb back into what he was talking about, and so the longer the second session needs to be. At this stage we invite the client to elaborate anything that he feels he left out previously, to correct any mistakes that he thinks we have made in coding and representing what he said and tell us about any bits that, while they might be fair representations of what he said, he does not want to see revealed to his colleagues as being what he said.

However, constraints of time, the problem-helper's energy levels and in some cases money, may mean that the problem-helper chooses to work with the whole team from the beginning. In this case, the process may start with the consultant in a team meeting which has been called to discuss the nature of the problem. We often try to make this something outside the normal run of activity of the team, for example by taking them away from their usual meeting place and by making sure that it is a helper and not the team leader who is in the chair: this last point may, as we said in Chapter 5, be influenced by how much the leader is inclined and able to play a helper-like chairman role, rather than being embroiled in the content of the discussions of the team.

MANAGING THE FIRST MEETING

If it is necessary to work with the team as a whole, or a sub-group of it, then the problem-helper has to consider how to ensure, as far as possible, that something is learned about the way each individual sees the situation which they are brought together to discuss. One way of providing a structure to help in this, is, at the beginning of the meeting, to ask each member of the team to write down on a card those things which he sees as most important, or is most 'fussed about', when he thinks about the particular problem label which the helper will have been given already by those with whom the intervention was arranged. This activity can be explained to the team in terms of different members of the team seeing the problem label in different ways and that it is important to try and discover the concerns and beliefs of each member of the team.

Then, each person, in turn, on a round-robin basis, is asked to call out one of the statements or concepts he has written down and the helper writes these up on a large flip chart in a circle around the central problem label. As each person calls out what he has written down, the helper can ask for an elaboration of its particular meaning through requesting the psychological opposite. In Figure 6.1 is an example of part of a concept map around the problem label 'more successful new product development'.

Drawing a concept map in this way gives the helper some understanding of similarities and differences in the concerns and beliefs of the members of the team, and also reduces the domination of the direction of discussion by one or two vocally powerful individuals.

In the example a helper could construct certain clusters from the ideas represented on the map, e.g. about team working, the concern with existing business, and the lack of direction from senior management. Often helpers will see clusters of ideas that they think represent shared areas of concern among some of the members of the team, albeit with different or conflicting beliefs. One such topic area can be the basis for further discussion, and a good idea is to start with one mentioned by several members of the team. Choosing one of the constructs within this topic area, the next stage is to ask people to talk about the significance of this particular aspect of the situation.

During this process we would recommend the problem-helper to code and

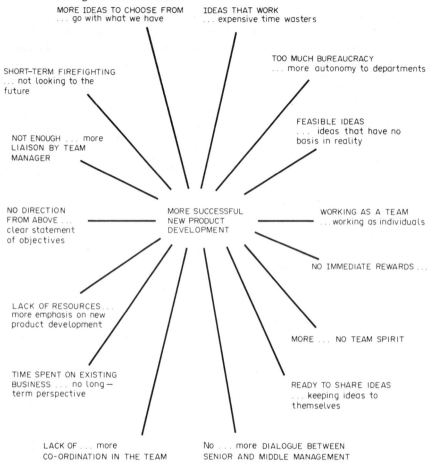

MORE IDEAS TO CHOOSE FROM
... go with what we have

IDEAS THAT WORK
... expensive time wasters

TOO MUCH BUREAUCRACY
... more autonomy to departments

SHORT-TERM FIREFIGHTING
... not looking to the
future

FEASIBLE IDEAS
... ideas that have no
basis in reality

NOT ENOUGH ... more
LIAISON BY TEAM
MANAGER

NO DIRECTION
FROM ABOVE ...
clear statement
of objectives

MORE SUCCESSFUL
NEW PRODUCT
DEVELOPMENT

WORKING AS A TEAM
... working as individuals

NO IMMEDIATE REWARDS ...

LACK OF RESOURCES...
more emphasis on new
product development

MORE ... NO TEAM SPIRIT

TIME SPENT ON EXISTING
BUSINESS ... no long—
term perspective

READY TO SHARE IDEAS
... keeping ideas to
themselves

LACK OF ... more
CO-ORDINATION IN THE TEAM

No ... more DIALOGUE BETWEEN
SENIOR AND MIDDLE MANAGEMENT

FIG. 6.1.

represent theories as they are being articulated. It is bad enough trying to keep hold of the complexity articulated by one individual in a meeting. With a number of different individuals where the diversity of ideas is likely to be greater and the theories of one individual spark off more ideas from someone else, it is virtually impossible without taking some kind of 'notes' in this way. If these are done on a flip chart in front of the team the members of the team are themselves enabled to hold on to the different theories of different individuals as they are expressed, which would otherwise be lost in a wide-ranging discussion, to relate the ideas expressed at different times in the discussion and gain immediate 'feedback' which many individuals appear to find rewarding. We have often found that the members of a team express both surprise and pleasure at the way in which so many ideas have been collected over a relatively short period of time about a situation using 'on-the-spot' cognitive mapping. This method also provides a structure for the meeting as a map becomes a focus for elaboration in particular directions and making explicit the relationships, similarities and differences across perspectives.

Doing 'on-the-spot' coding becomes much easier with practice. However, it will never be as 'tidy' and visually neat as a map which has been carefully drawn with an eye to appearance, spacing and concept clusters. This does not matter when you are representing the views of other people about a situation which is meaningful and important to them; matters of tidiness are pretty unimportant so long as the map is legible. What is important is to get down the ideas and beliefs as they are articulated. There is always an opportunity to 'tidy up' the map and check on understanding later.

Thus, for example, someone might say in answer to the question "Why is it important to you that you work as a team rather than working as individuals?", that "if we worked better as a team we would be ready to share our ideas, and then we would have not only, probably, more ideas but also better ideas". This could be coded as shown in Figure 6.2.

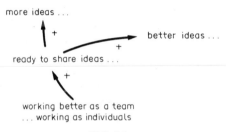

FIG. 6.2.

At this point another member of the team might say: "I am not sure I agree with that. When people share ideas there isn't the same commitment to carry the idea through so really they aren't better ideas, because nothing gets done properly". This could be added as seen in Figure 6.3.

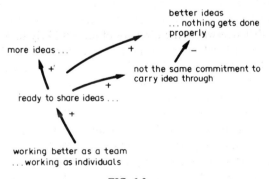

FIG. 6.3.

The notion of "nothing gets done properly" seems to represent a psychological opposite for the second speaker to "better ideas". However, the first speaker may have a different construct and at this stage it would be helpful to check with him what he means by "better ideas". He might say that for him, "better ideas are those which are not merely fanciful, having no basis in reality". This is clearly a different construct from the other and should be expressed on the map as such.

Two members of the team have expressed conflicting ideas. At this early stage it is important that these differences be expressed in the map and, as far as possible, the team should be encouraged to leave aside negotiation about which is the 'better' theory until later, when there is a much fuller picture available for debate and analysis.

The other question which emerges in on-the-spot coding is the amount of time spent on requesting opposite poles. To keep repeating the question can become tedious after a while. However, if one does so initially, often members of a team begin to express alternatives on their own initiative, as they come to see the way mapping works. Thus, having coded in the way shown above, the helper can ask what are the opposites of "more ideas", which might be "not enough", and "ready to share ideas", which might be expressed in the same terms as are written already on the concept map, "keeping ideas to themselves." At this stage, the helper can move on to the team member who had originally expressed this construct on the concept map and ask him whether he had been thinking about the same things himself when he had suggested that construct. He might add "yes, that's one part of it. But the other aspect which I think is important is that it's not surprising that people tend to work as individuals when it's individuals who get a pat on the back, not teams." This would then be included in the map, and the speaker asked to say a little bit more about the explanations and implications of this state of affairs.

In this way, giving perhaps ten minutes to each team member to elaborate the meaning of the constructs he had expressed in the concept map, the problem-helper produces a cognitive map of what is being articulated. There will undoubtedly be relationships between many of the ideas expressed by the different individuals, and the problem-helper will be checking these during the meeting and putting in relationships across the map if they exist. However, despite this 'connecting' process it is likely that the map will be somewhat 'bitty', but greater elaboration along explanations and consequences of ideas can take place in the succeeding meetings, after the initial attempt to understand the range of theories across the team.

MERGING MAPS

At some point the helper who has chosen to work with individual team members first will wish to bring the team, or a sub-group of it, together. For this he will need to produce an aggregated map, representing the beliefs of the members of the team about the situation which they are prepared to reveal to one another.

In one case, for example, three members of a housing department wanted us to help them share their maps as they related to the housing investment programme. We already had a large map of the concepts of one of these people, which had sections relevant to this question, and we built maps individually in discussion with each of the other two. We also introduced a map of concepts that had been used for a previous year's housing investment programme document. We then wanted to merge these four maps together so that they could be explored by the team as if they were a single entity. We did this by merging some of the common concepts, and drawing links between others of the concepts on the different maps. We continued doing this until it was possible to explore the merged map as a whole without coming across cases where concepts which seemed as if they ought to have been linked, but because they came from different maps were not linked.

The larger the team whose maps are being merged, the more difficult it is to challenge the 'concept mergers' that are put in in order to make the connections. However, if the concepts are still in the words of the people who produced them, they seem able to own and explore and play with the maps, together with other members of their team, in a way which they find useful even if the relationships between the concepts have been tampered with to some considerable extent. Indeed, often it seems that a certain amount of tampering with the maps makes them much more interesting to the user team, and the members can become more engaged with work on a merged map than they would with work on their own individual maps.

MERGING CONCEPTS

Whether the helper has collected concepts by listening to team members individually or listening to them all together, he is likely sometimes to want to merge some of the concepts being used, in addition to any merging of maps that may have taken place if the initial concept collection was done individually. If he has talked to three people in a team in the accounts department, and they have all mentioned their beliefs about relationships with the marketing department, then often it is useful for members of a team to see a model in which the different beliefs which they have about such a concept are all represented together. Quite often this shows a richness and variety — contradiction even — in the beliefs of the members of a team which usually gets lost sight of in the process of reaching agreements. Keeping all these beliefs there together may be helpful for the team members in thinking about what they are doing. However, to bring these beliefs together requires that some of the concepts of different people be aggregated together, either by merging concepts so that one concept remains, or by drawing new links between the concepts of different persons.

In earlier chapters we have made the connection between the concepts that we map and the personal construct theories of Kelly. The concepts that people use in thinking about their situations are idiosyncratic, and we have observed that their meaning may be defined in a very individual context, and in relation to a psychological, rather than a logical, opposite. When we aggregate together the concepts of different persons we are choosing not to be governed by this argument, but rather by the opposing argument, which is that there is a degree of commonality between different persons' concepts, and that different persons do mean something of the same thing by similar words. The decision to merge such concepts is made on the basis of their meaning being so similar that there is no significant distortion resulting from merging them and the advantages of so doing in terms of reducing some of the complexity coming from the volume of data, make it worthwhile. Great care, however, is needed on the part of the helper to make sure that the concepts being merged really are seen as similar by his clients. In terms of understanding meaning, the helper is looking not only at the individual bipolar concepts, but also at their context in terms of related ideas. For example, in one case, several members of the editorial team of a magazine told us some of their beliefs about 'regular readers'. When it came to putting together a model for the team we might have merged these into one concept if we had not happened to notice that the context around them suggested that the different team members might have different meanings for the words. In the next team meeting we checked this impression, and found that it was in fact the case; one person meant by 'regular' those readers who bought the magazine every week and had an order for it at a newsagent. Another person meant those who bought it almost every week if there was one left when they remembered, and who probably ended up buying three a month, while another person turned out to mean those who read the magazine at least once a month. These people had been talking about regular readers as if they all meant the same thing for years. It was only the context of their concepts, seen in maps, which finally revealed the misunderstanding.

It is cases such as this that have led us to prefer to do most of our merging in the company of the owners of the concepts concerned. This is not always possible, particularly if there are large numbers of maps that have to be brought together before presenting an aggregated map back to a team. In this case we often make a note to check particular mergers if we do not feel very much confidence in them. Mergers are very often suggested when helpers are listening to a team together, where one member will say something, and another member will say, "Isn't that the same as . . . ?" This may be a helpful merging activity which can enable more of the linkages between different persons' beliefs and concepts to become visible, but the helper should accept the suggestion only with some caution. Most of us, when we are told that we are saying the same as someone else, tend to feel that we were actually trying to say something a little bit different, and that part of the richness of what we were saying is lost if it is taken to be no more than repetition. It should not be too easily accepted that, because one person says that two concepts can be merged, and the owners of both those concepts agree, that there is no loss of richness involved in the merger. Unless there has been some discussion of beliefs around those concepts, the owners of them may not even know the difference between their positions.

MERGING CHAINS OF CONCEPTS

We often find that a concept seems to connect with several other concepts, and not only the one in connection with which it was first mentioned. As new concepts are added either the helper or members of the team may think of possible connections with other existing concepts on the map, in some cases several other concepts.

This leads the helper to merging chains of concepts. In Figures 6.4 and 6.5 we show two sets of beliefs from two different individuals which could be merged.

The choice of which concept of merged concepts remains within the map is relatively arbitrary or depends upon which the problem-helper believes to capture most. In some cases merging can mean pairing one half of one concept with the other half of the other, as in a couple of cases here. If the problem-helper does not wish to merge in certain cases then concepts that are similar can be placed side by side linked connotatively (see Chapter 4 for the significance of this); or can be merged for the purposes of a chain or beliefs but the 'removed' concept retained by means of a connotative link, as with "no . . . some team spirit" in

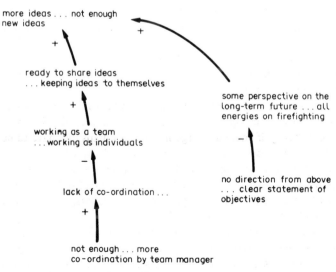

FIG. 6.4.

FIG. 6.5.

the Figure 6.6 example. Connotative links can be usefully used in several ways: to indicate a close similarity between concepts which, however, the problem-helper does not wish to merge; suggesting that there may be some relationship between ideas, such as in the constructs about time and energy in the above example; where the problem-helper feels that there is a causal link between theories in two different individual maps but does not feel able to put this in before discussing it with the team.

GROUPING IN TEAMS

We have discussed in Chapter 4 the notion of grouping concepts as a way of sorting them and of enabling people to find their way about them. In the very large maps which tend to result from model building in teams, the significance of grouping becomes even greater. Because of the merging of concepts and the introduction of extra links, the connectivity of concepts tends to be rather high in team maps, and so exploring the concepts connected to only one or two concepts may provide a considerable amount of material for a team.

The helper should analyse the content and structure of individual maps first to decide which clusters of concepts appear to represent different areas of concern, asking "What things does this person appear to be particularly fussed about; what other ideas are connotatively linked to those things or have consequences for them?" Having done this, and seen how areas of concern are related to one another, the helper then compares the individual maps to see if there are mutual areas of concern among the members of the team, even if the content may be

An aggregation

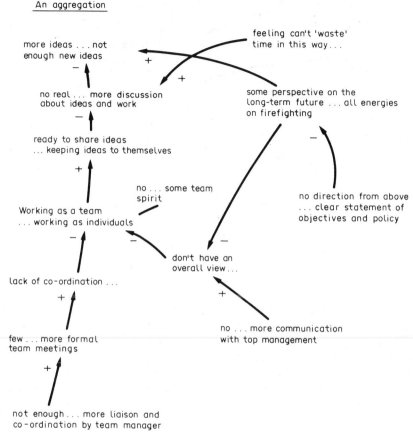

FIG. 6.6.

different, or conflicting, in detail. He can then merge these areas of concern, or 'groups' of concepts. Thus, returning to our example, the helper could group into one merged area of concern all the groups of concepts in the individual maps which had as their key concept something to do with the idea of "working as a team rather than working as individuals".

However, the helper would do well to be very cautious, and if he is not very confident about the similarity of certain groups, he would best leave the merged map having a larger number of groups and then explore similarities and differences further with the team.

As we have discussed in Chapter 2, the individual definition of issues is idiosyncratic, and what one person regards as relevant to an issue another may well not. This can be very illuminating and helpful in team discussion, but it will usually work best if the team members have done their own grouping and made their own judgements as to which of their concepts is relevant to a particular issue.

ANALYSIS, FEEDBACK AND ELABORATION

Because team maps tend to be so much more complicated than individual maps, some of the functions that an analyst can perform upon maps can be even more helpful for teams than for individuals. For example, an analyst might set out to discover feedback loops which arise from the team map, to see if bringing together the thinking of different members of the team suggests any vicious circles which it might be well for the members to be aware of. Similarly, exploring some particular policy, an analyst might do work, possibly using a computer, to trace through paths and consequences of certain policy actions.

Some of the most interesting learning from looking at maps comes from the occasions where there are both positive and negative routes between two concepts. With a large and involved map this may be difficult to spot with the naked eye, certainly in the heat of group discussion, but such links may be discovered by the analyst studying the map, or using computer assistance to help him search for such indicators of likely problems.

When feeding back the merged map the helper will need to give some overview of the model as a whole first of all. Without identifying individuals' ideas, he will explain briefly what seemed to have emerged as areas of concern for the team members, possibly using a 'hierarchy' diagram of the relationship between areas of concern, similar to that shown in Chapter 4. One of these areas will then become the focus for the first more detailed feedback, using the map to show the different theories which have been expressed, some of which may involve conflicts and contradictions, pointing out any feedback loops which may exist, bringing attention to concepts and relationships which seem to be particularly significant in terms of points for action. (Each area of concern can be set out on a separate flip chart sheet for feedback.) Which area the detailed discussion begins with will depend on which the helper sees as most significant, in terms of general concern expressed by members of the team.

The helper will then begin to address some of the beliefs which appear to represent conflicts between members of the team. The map becomes a focus for discussion and negotiation, and the helper will reflect the elaboration and modification that occurs through on-the-spot coding to the existing visual map.

Case Study

Jenny still was not sure exactly how to handle this next stage. It was a tricky one. She did not know whether she had done the right thing in leaving Ian out of it. On the one hand, the games that were bound to go on between the marketing managers, with Justin desperately trying to prove his competence, and between them and Alan would be difficult enough to handle, without Ian's presence complicating matters. She still didn't know what exactly Ian wanted from her involvement other than a change of direction in new product development; she suspected, however, that he also wanted to get something over on Alan and probably to show his mettle as the new dynamic boss, which was an added unpredictable factor for her to handle in what might already be a high-risk situation. On the other hand if he was presented with a *fait accompli* that he didn't like the consequences could be disastrous. However, it was too late now. She'd have to play the timing of his involvement a little bit by ear, depending on what emerged with the others.

The other question was how to manage the process of a group meeting to bring all the ideas together with the others. If there was one thing that had come out from her discussion with each of the marketing managers, it was that they were all totally wrapped up in their own areas of responsibility. Not that this was either surprising or wrong, but it meant that either they would not be in the least bit interested in those parts of the group meeting that weren't to do with them, or they might become extremely defensive or angry if someone else — Justin for example — started making helpful remarks about what they might do with their own products! At the same time there was one significant commonality — John, Peter and Justin had all talked about the need to keep up with new technology, although exactly what this implied in terms of the kind of technology was as yet unclear. It might be that they all meant the same kind of development, or it might be that their visions were so different that if some kind of joint decision about new-product development was to be made, then they would have to work through together the ramifications of their different ideas. And if they were all convinced that some radical departure was needed, then it would perhaps be easier to move Alan in that direction if they were persuaded by the weight of their joint arguments. She felt that Alan was the sort of person who could be prepared to change his mind if he was presented with what he saw as reasonable arguments. Another alternative might be to get the marketing managers together with Alan on a one-to-one basis. This would at least mean that they were both talking about things that interested them and might reduce some of the more unhelpful dynamics of a group meeting.

She decided that before she made up her mind finally she would go back to John, Peter and Justin, show them their maps both to 'test the water' a bit more and to explore what they meant by new technology. She felt she would have had to do something like that anyway — even if it involved a fairly quick meeting — so that they could see what a map looked like and thus have some ideas of what a joint meeting around a qualitative model might mean. When arranging to do this she explained to each of them how she had come by the qualitative model. She reminded them that when talking to her about the figures for the quantitative model they had expressed some ideas that they could not put numbers on but still seemed quite important to thinking about new products, and that it seemed worthwhile modelling these too, but in a qualitative form. Before she did this though, she wanted to check that she had got things right, and to look at one or two things in a bit more detail. She also added that she had cleared this with Ian.

(At least this might dispel ideas that she was wasting their time, and the careful use of a little muscle every now and then was sometimes a good idea.)

None of the meetings turned out to be very long, but they were useful nonetheless. John was still relatively offhand, but he was not antagonistic and seemed quite impressed with the idea of explicitly modelling qualitative beliefs. He did develop some ideas that had not been there before — about the possibility of there being more market synergy between the newer up-market lines and his own. It became clearer that he was not thinking of any drastic change in technology but more of an up-dating on the lines Alan had suggested, to increase their price competitiveness and the addition of their own plastics capability. Justin just continued dishing out his 'bright young man' script about the need to sharpen up on their marketing expertise — but what was interesting was that both his and John's map shared an interest in a greater 'attack' on the consumer, rather than on the distributor side of the market. Peter was the surprise. After not having said much in previous discussions he became quite animated and began to elaborate on the need to move into computerized industrial valves. She saw Peter last and by then she had become clearer in her own mind that the best way of proceeding might be to bring John and Justin together with Alan and keep Peter out of it to talk separately to Alan. It would be pretty easy to explain in terms of the distinction between consumer and industrial products, and this arrangement might solve the problem of Ian's role, and explain his absence from the meeting. If Alan could present something on both aspects of the new-product development programme then Ian could have the opportunity to develop some strategy relating the two, calling in the others with Alan at a later stage.

The meetings had all taken place within a week (the trip to Switzerland had been a short one) so Alan had not been left too long since her last meeting with him, and she had explained to him that she had been using maps to collect some of the qualitative ideas of the others. He had looked a little surprised but hadn't objected and when she suggested the possibility of two meetings, one with John and Justin and one with Peter, he had merely grinned and said "O.K., why not, it might be very useful". She had the sneaking suspicion that he was more politically astute than she had first imagined, and had worked out what she was up to. "Why didn't he mind?", she wondered.

Justin was predictably delighted at the idea of a meeting where he presumably felt he could start to have some impact on events and get some Brownie points with Ian. Jenny wondered how much Ian had told him of his feelings about Alan on their trip together. She would have to make sure that he did not start trying to trample over Alan — but John and Alan would probably keep him under control. She told him that she would put his map together with the others to produce an aggregated model, and checked with him that "presumably you would prefer me to leave out the personal comments about Ian and Alan". She didn't want them in anyway, and he agreed.

John also seemed quite pleased at the idea of a meeting, even with Justin, and Peter was also prepared to go along with the idea. "Yes, it's probably about time we had a look at where we're going", he said. She made a mental note that it was probably that meeting which was going to be the most difficult.

The next stage was to aggregate the maps – Alan's with Peter's and Justin's and Alan's again with John's.

To prepare for the feedback with Alan, John and Justin, and Alan and Peter, Jenny used the computer and the COPE software package to help. Although the computer was able to administrate and analyse the data quickly and flexibly it is not essential to the sort of preparation Jenny was undertaking. In general the more individuals' maps that have to be aggregated the more benefits there are from using COPE. In this case Jenny was aggregating four relatively small models and so COPE was not essential but rather an advantage.

As Jenny was pursuing the project she had been constructing each individual model using the computer. At this stage she had a model for each of Alan, Peter, John and Justin. Her first task was to create a new model with the appropriate models added to one another and similar concepts merged so that the models were interconnected. These are two obvious ways of merging aspects of a model. Firstly, two concepts may have very similar verbal tags, even though they mean different things in the sense of being set within different belief contexts. In this case one of the two concepts is chosen as 'most complete' and the other merged into it so that one concept is lost but the relationships are held as context to the remaining concept. Secondly, concepts in one person's map may clearly relate to those in another person's map, and so relationships or connotative links can be inserted to show this linking of ideas.

For example, Alan had been discussing "lower selling price" and John "keeping prices down rather than following costs". It seemed to Jenny that little violence would be done to the sense of what Alan was discussing if Alan's concept were merged into that of John. (In the computer this is easily done by giving the command 'm9=-16' which says make the inversion of concept 16, which belongs to Alan, the same as concept 9, which belongs to John; the computer will automatically carry across the relationships belonging to 16 to concept 9.) Similarly Jenny thought there was a link between John's concept "invest in up-to-date technology rather than keep old inefficient plant" and Alan's concept "technological innovation rather than stagnation of products". Jenny linked the two with a +ve signed causal belief link.

A very helpful way of looking for links between maps comes from doing word searches on the list of concepts. Thus, for example, Jenny asked the computer to search for all concepts with the word 'marketing' in them. By doing so she was able to spot a potential link between Alan's comment that "Ian was brought up in marketing" and Justin's belief in "Ian's enormously helpful marketing expertise". She linked Alan's comment to that of Justin by a causal relationship with positive signification. Jenny also did word searches for 'sales',

'Ian', 'image', 'tech', 'advert' and 'merchant'. She spotted several other links by observation, such as the causal link between "Alan needs to know what I need" and "freeze development".

Gradually the aggregated map became a merged map so that the ideas and beliefs of the three persons could be seen and understood in relation to each other. In some circumstances Jenny may have chosen to add her own views of the issue by first constructing her own map (she often uses a dialogue version of COPE to help her express her own views in the form of a cognitive map in the computer). Her ideas then become a basis for introducing an intelligent outsider's view and analysis in a manner that is negotiative, and seen in the context of the views of her client group. In this case she had decided that it was too early in the proceedings to do anything other than try to facilitate negotiation amongst the client participants.

After aggregation and merging she finished up with a model too large to feed back to them in one go. She was also aware that there were several 'problems' within the 'issue' they were addressing. She saw her next job as trying to locate these clusters of ideas and then find a way of feeding them back as groups of ideas which are interconnected. To do this she decided to use a rule of thumb which seems to work well when analysing cognitive maps: she searched for those concepts which were most central because they were the ones with the most explanations, consequences and links with others. Using the computer this is a simple request and the computer presents a list in order of 'centrality'. Using these as 'key' concepts she then let the computer automatically form groups of concepts following the method discussed in Chapter 4.

Looking at the interconnection between these 'areas of concern' produced the first map she intended to feed back (shown as Figure 6.7). We can see

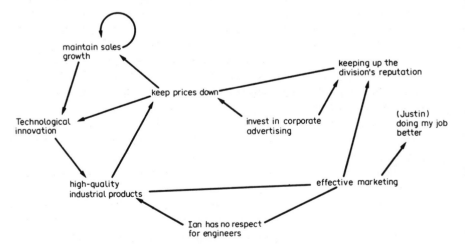

FIG. 6.7. Relationship between areas of concern.

that there are nine clusters each interconnected with others. We may suppose that each cluster is a problem arena which, if tackled on its own, would produce ramifications for other problem arenas. However, Jenny was a little concerned about the existence of two very personal problem areas: "Ian has no respect for engineers" and "Justin doing his job better". She wondered whether it would be helpful to feed back such 'illegitimate' problems. She concluded that it would be wholly unhelpful to ignore the problem about Ian as this was a keystone of the product development issue as seen by Alan; but decided to make 'opaque' the cluster about Justin.

She could now produce maps for each of the clusters (the computer will type the concepts in a sensible layout leaving the analyst to draw the arrows). However, she needed to look at other possible maps that could facilitate debate. She got the computer to locate all those concepts that appeared in several groups; any such concept was potentially important because of its contribution to several different problem areas. "Ian brought up in marketing" was in five of the nine groups, more than any other concept. She also got the computer to search for all feedback loops in the aggregated model; there were four loops, each of them positive (that is potentially vicious circles). Finally, she asked the computer to search for any conflicting paths, that is circumstances where one set of arguments from one concept to another conflict with the outcome of another set of arguments to and from the same concepts. In this aggregated map she discovered one conflicting path from "recession" to 'the future of the company".

Jenny now had nine maps of areas of concern, a map showing the inter-relationship of these areas of concern, a map of loops, a map of the conflicting path, and a map showing the concepts immediately surrounding "Ian brought up in marketing". She also produced a list of all concepts and a set of self-adhesive labels, one for each concept, which she could use to quickly make her own maps if necessary. She normally tried to produce an A4 booklet for each participant which would contain the maps she was intending to use during the meeting. She thought the same method was appropriate in this case and so carefully chose which maps to use and deleted those concepts she felt would not help 'public' debate. Figures 6.8, 6.9, and 6.10 are examples of those she intended to use. She completed her preparation by drawing each map on to a flip chart which was to be the centre of attention during the meeting.

She began the meeting with John, Justin and Alan by explaining again how she had attempted to put the ideas together and how they seemed to fall into three different areas. She had already decided that she wanted to look at the feedback loops with them first, and so after her introductory explanation immediately suggested that the loops were interesting. At this point Alan broke in – he pointed delightedly to the cost-pricing issue. "Yes, there we have it", he exclaimed. "We've got to keep up with alloy technology otherwise we'll fall right behind on competitiveness, and once these foreign products get a hold we're sunk." John was looking cautious, and Jenny was just about to ask him

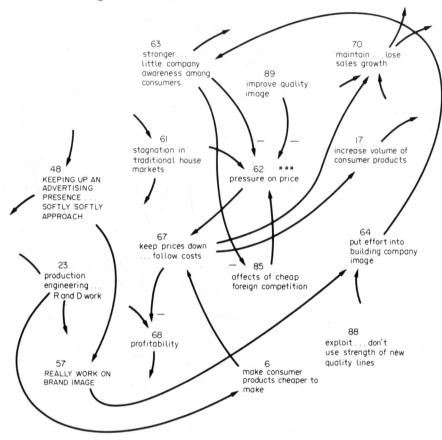

FIG. 6.8. Group 7 "pressure on price".

what he thought when Justin blurted out; "Yes, that's all very well, but look what it says here" (pointing to his own concepts). "What about the question of keeping up our reputation and here — 'just chugging along'. We've got to move with the times, and that means more than just doing the same thing cheaper." Both Alan and John glared at him — they obviously didn't like him very much, and Jenny felt that she might well have to help him out of it — his ideas weren't that bad, he just did not know how to present them. "What do you think?", she asked John, refocusing on the cost question, "There seems to be some contradiction here on whether if you moved into plastics unit costs would be more or less expensive." "I agree that the price of oil is a problem", he said, "and I also agree that we shouldn't abandon our existing foundry skills altogether but I do think that in absolute terms plastic products are cheaper . . . and it's where our future lies. Consumers expect and want plastic products, and they

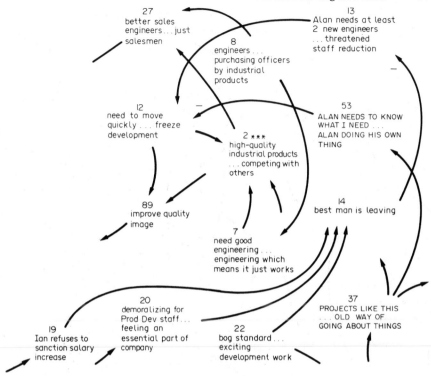

FIG. 6.9. Group 2 "high-quality industrial products".

want absolutely cheaper products, even if a small segment is prepared to pay for the up-market end." "Yes, but while that may be so now", Alan added, "the price of oil is going to continue to soar and this situation is going to stay this way. There are plenty of examples of where products which were once too expensive to contemplate are now feasible because the price of oil has made the alternatives too costly."

In the meantime Jenny was adding these beliefs to the maps. She found that she did not have to do much intervening – the discussion moved quite naturally to the various implications of the different scenarios with both Alan and John debating without apparently needing to ride their own hobby horses. Even Justin settled down and made suggestions that the others listened to. After about an hour and a half, the maps had developed by many more concepts, although there still wasn't much agreement about where to go next. Alan had however begun to think about, and throw out ideas about, a number of possible new-product avenues. His commitment to improving the existing taps was beginning to change. Yet it was also becoming clear to all of them that they were unlikely to get much further without putting some numbers on some of the ideas. As

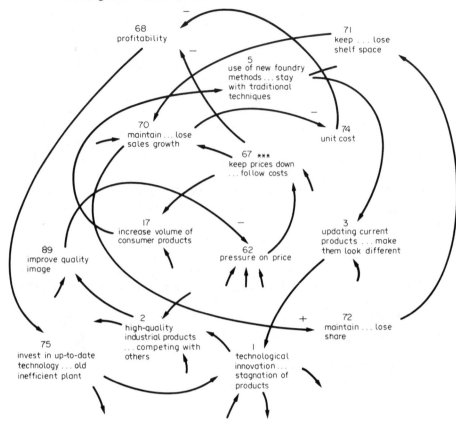

FIG. 6.10. Loops.

Alan said, "We really won't know until we make some estimates of what moving into plastics would mean – not just in terms of product and client costs but also in terms of the new skills we'd have to buy in". It was at this stage that Jenny suggested they stop, and that perhaps that was where they should go next. They all agreed, and it was John who proposed that "I think we should all have a think about the numbers side before we meet again".

The meeting with Peter was considerably less successful. Jenny was surprised. She had expected that Alan and Peter were similar enough, 'down to earth', to get on quite well. She realized afterwards that perhaps she had not paid enough attention to Peter's scathing comments about Alan, although there was probably not much she could have done about their interpersonal dynamics anyway. Peter had started by launching fairly early on in the meeting into a personal attack on Alan. "The trouble with you, Alan, is you can't see what's in front of your own nose. We're living in the world of the micro-chip whether we like it or not, and if we don't get in on it, we're going to be left completely behind." He got up and walked over to the flip chart on which the model was laid out. He pointed to it — "these things aren't separate — non-aqueous flows are an important market opportunity for us but it's micro-technology that we need to get into". Alan looked stunned and hurt. Jenny decided that she had better give him time to recover and turning to Peter asked "O.K., let's have a look at that. What might happen if we don't move into that area?" Peter exploded again. "It's obvious — we'll just go down the Swanee. I am already getting feedback from our customers that they don't think Leakey is what it used to be." Jenny tried again. "Can you be a bit more precise . . . perhaps give an estimate of what might happen to sales in the next three years?"

She was beginning to feel that perhaps this would not do Alan any harm. Shock treatment might be quite useful so long as Alan's ego was given some resuscitation later.

She let Peter continue, looking at various aspects of moving into micro-technology, and he quietened down particularly when Alan began to ask Peter questions, listening to the answers and not expressing his own evaluations. After an hour Jenny decided to call the meeting to a halt, wondering what on earth to do next. Peter had stopped being acrimonious, Alan hadn't rejected his ideas out of hand, but it had all been a bit too near the knuckle for her liking. She felt she might have damaged her relationship with Alan permanently.

7

Coping with Quantity

Many of the problems belonging to individuals in organizations involve an interest in the numerical implications of particular policies, even if such concerns represent no more (and no less) than legitimating labels for the problems. Costs of production, distribution, promotion and manpower, levels of turnover and profitability are a few obvious examples of factors which an individual in an industrial organization may wish, or be required to take account of. The client may introduce rough and ready numbers from the start. An interest in exploring some of the quantitative implications of the problem may come at a much later stage of exploring and evaluating a qualitative model, or perhaps solely when considering how best to persuade other people to adopt certain recommendations. Whatever their origin, if quantitative elements are seen as important aspects of a problem a helper and client are working on, then it would be as inappropriate to ignore them as we argued it is to ignore non-quantifiable or primarily qualitative aspects.

The following section is for those who are interested in the process by which a cognitive map can be the basis for producing a quantitative model. To do this we shall use a specific example and consider how a cognitive map can be the basis of an influence diagram for a Systems Dynamics model.[1] The use of the word 'process' is deliberate. Our concern is not with the relatively easy technical transformation of an influence diagram to a Systems Dynamics flow diagram and a 'Dynamo' computer model. For this we refer you to the text below.[2] We wish rather to set quantitative modelling within the approach to problem-helping that we have outlined in the rest of this text, and to consider some of what we regard as the most important issues surrounding so doing. It is also important to state that we are not proposing a Systems Dynamics model as the only appropriate form of quantitative model, nor that the discussion here is only relevant to Systems Dynamics models.

We use Systems Dynamics models because they take account of the dynamic consequences of perceived feedback loops which are otherwise quite difficult to handle, and because they are relatively easy to construct using influence diagrams

[1] See the seminal work by Forrester (1961, 1971).
[2] A useful text on the practical aspects of Systems Dynamics modelling is by Coyle (1977).

which are similar in form to cognitive maps. It is important, however, to distinguish between influence diagrams in Systems Dynamics modelling as they are typically used, to model the underlying structure of some 'objective' reality and cognitive maps which are intended to represent, using his own language and theories, the 'problem — reality' defined by the client. A similar point should also be made about the distinction between flow charts or network diagrams, which are intended to model a set of events or processes in a strictly logical, sequential manner, and cognitive maps which may or may not do so, depending on the way in which the client sees his world. The latter distinction does not imply that listening to a client by means of a cognitive map cannot be used to construct at some stage, if required, a flow chart or network diagram; and this activity would almost certainly require some restructuring to satisfy certain logical or computational requirements, as is also usually necessary when moving from a cognitive map to a Systems Dynamics model.

We shall take as an example the situation whereby a consultant has been asked by the advertisement manager and editor of a trade journal to assist them to consider ways of reviving the fortunes of the journal. It has been steadily declining in profitability and circulation for the last few years. The resort to consultancy help has come at the instigation of senior management in the large publishing corporation which owns the journal, and it is clear from the first meeting with the two clients that they believe the journal will be discontinued if they cannot reverse its decline. Thus the problem labelled "need to reverse the decline in circulation and profitability of this journal" is one likely to be characterized by a considerable degree of personal anxiety, and several different meanings to the people involved in terms of the personal implications of failure or success. Qualitative and quantitative aspects are likely to be closely linked.

DECIDING TO QUANTIFY

Let us assume that Figure 7.1 shows part of the map constructed after the first meeting with the team. (It is adapted from a project similar to the one we are describing here.) It shows several feedback loops, truly 'vicious' circles, the content of which would not be unrecognizable in many different product fields, and including the feedback loop relating journal size to circulation which traditionally exists in periodical publishing. It is clear that there are some concepts which are readily quantifiable, such as 'circulation', 'number of editorial pages', 'issue size', 'new sales', and so on. Let us also assume that in the discussion with the team its members have assigned numbers to the concepts about circulation, pages and issue size, with some disagreements about the 'correct' numbers to be given, and to no others. The helper, however, feels that further quantification is likely to be critical to exploring the particular circumstances of this journal and devising satisfactory policies. For example, he wonders what is the relationship between the number of new introductions and the budget for the sales

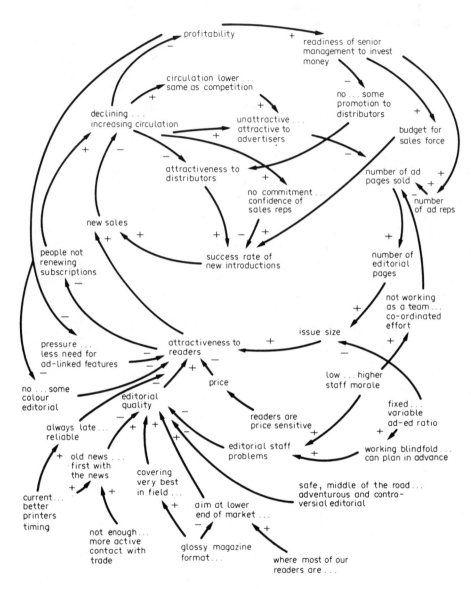

FIG. 7.1.

force?; what is the success rate for new introductions currently?; what proportion of readers are not renewing their subscriptions?; what is the relationship between number of advertising salesmen and the number of ad pages sold?; how many readers does 'most of our readers' represent?, and so on. There are several feed-back loops and he believes that there will probably be a need to explore the dynamics of these. His own construction of the problem therefore includes more quantitative aspects than the team has shown interest in initially and he believes that a dynamic quantitative model is likely to be helpful.

The decision he must make, therefore, is whether or not to encourage the team to think in more quantitative terms. We would argue, within the negotiative (rather than purely empathetic) paradigm that we use, whereby helper and client negotiate a problem construction which they both feel committed to working upon, he has every right to, and indeed should, do so. However, if he is to avoid the team being 'turned off' by his problem construction, then he must proceed with great care.

Thus if he decides to encourage a move towards a quantitative model he must consider what concepts in the map should or could be quantified by the team members. We have suggested that some concepts are readily quantifiable, although it is likely that there will be some concepts for which no 'hard' date is available, or the team disbelieves this data, and the helper will be working with the sub-jective estimates of the team. If the concept of quantification is broadened to include the thinking by which some estimation, by some sort of measure, is made of the weight, size, amount, probability of occurrence, of things, and their effects upon each other, then in principle many other concepts may be regarded as also quantifiable — for example 'editorial quality', 'attractiveness to readers and advertisers', 'readiness to invest', 'confidence' and so on. We are, however, referring here to quantification involving the assignment of numbers and numerical weights to things and their relationships within an approach which attempts to use this process as a means of capturing as richly and accurately as possible the meaning of a person's image of his world. Thus with respect to quantification, the test for us is that the meaning of concepts and relationships for an individual should be enriched and distorted as little as possible by the assignment of numbers, and that if there are distortions numbers should be used only when their usefulness outweighs the disadvantages of distortion.

For example, we may suppose that few people would consider it helpful or meaningful to quantify the concept 'adventurous rather than safe editorial' or would wish to define a precise numerical relationship between 'editorial quality' and 'staff problems' in a form such as '20% less staff problems' would lead to '30% more editorial quality'. It is, however, likely that there will be certain operational indicators of the meaning of these concepts and their relationships which it will be extremely useful to explore. Thus, for example, the nature of the relationship between editorial quality and staff problems may be expressed in terms of 'fewer rows with the advertising department about ad-related features would mean we would feel upset less often and be able to concentrate more on our job — writing good editorial'. Similarly, although the concept of 'attractiveness to readers' will be needed in the Systems Dynamics model as an intermediary variable within a loop, through which various policy variables 'enter' and affect the dynamics of a loop, it may be extremely difficult for the team members to feel they can give a sensible and meaningful numerical estimate of the relationship between 'editorial quality' and 'attractiveness to readers'. They may, however, feel able to answer the question, "If you were to carry out this policy of aiming at the lower end of the market, with more adventurous editorial, how many readers do you think might not cancel their subscription who otherwise would were the journal left unchanged?" It is then up to the helper to do the necessary computations for the quantitative model.

THE PROCESS OF NEGOTIATION

The helper has to decide when to introduce more strongly and negotiatively his interest in further quantification. He would probably begin to do so at the stage of feeding back the map constructed during the first meeting, having first also converted the map into an influence diagram.[3] It is important to do this at this early stage, because it assists the helper to decide what questions he needs to ask the team in order to produce the Systems Dynamics model, although it will undoubtedly be modified as a consequence of discussion.

The influence diagram from Figure 7.1 is shown in Figure 7.2 and it can be seen that the transition is a relatively easy one particularly since many of the concepts in the map are already capable of being expressed numerically.

It is, however, worth noting how some meaning is inevitably lost by the translation to a monotonic concept of the idea that 'an increasing circulation' is attractive to advertisers 'while a declining circulation' is unattractive to them. In the influence diagram the concepts of 'attractiveness to advertisers, distributors', 'commitment of the sales force' and 'readiness of senior management to invest', have been dispensed with altogether. They are important within the overall problem construction and must not be forgotten. They are, however, difficult to quantify and unnecessary arithmetically and so can be ignored within the quantitative model.[4] Since the potential reader market will not be infinite, relationships between potential reader market and circulation, not explicit in the cognitive map, have also been included.

As he moves from an empathetic to a negotiative stance in feeding back the cognitive map to the team, the helper will probably concentrate upon the nature and significance of its feedback loops. As the discussion progresses and concepts

---

[3] See Coyle, *op. cit.*, chapter 3.
[4] See Alonzo (1968) for a discussion of the danger inherent in attempts to quantify with numerous variables.

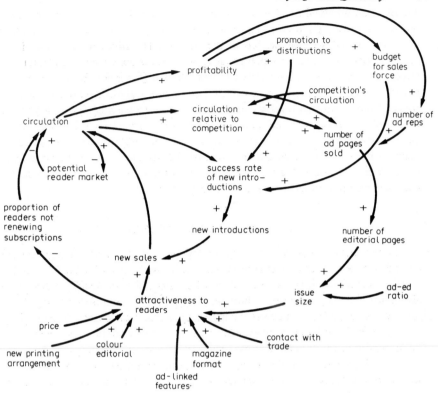

FIG. 7.2.

and relationships common to the cognitive map and influence diagram are discussed, he would begin to encourage the members of the group to make rough estimates of the numbers involved.

Thus, for example, about the relationship between issue size and attractiveness to readers, he could ask something like the following: "Your current average size is x pages. What size would you like to see it? If you managed to have an issue size such as this, what sort of reduction/increase might you get in the number of people not renewing subscriptions/new buyers coming in. . . . What about the next feasible page size above/below this, would this have a greater/lesser effect", and so on. He could then construct a graph of the estimated effects of different issues' sizes upon the sales levels. In undertaking a process such as this we have found it helpful to pay attention to individuality by asking each person to first of all write down his estimates before announcing them, and then, on a 'round-robin' basis, each person to call out his estimate which could be written up on a chart or board. This can then be a basis for discussion and negotiation to arrive at a mutually acceptable estimate. Should there be uncertainty or reluctance among the members of the team about a single estimate, then another approach is to ask for three assumptions: high, low and expected to work with these.

Throughout this process the helper would pay considerable attention to encouraging the team members to feel that their own and others' subjective estimates, even if very different, were legitimate reflections of each individual's knowledge about his organization and his market, to be worthy of consideration, discussion and negotiation. He would be careful not to force the team members to produce numbers which they were clearly unhappy to produce. Thus a strong resistance by some individuals to giving certain estimates could be handled by not pressing further and suggesting that the individuals concerned think about this particular aspect before the next meeting, if possible researching any data they feel might be relevant within the organization.

ELABORATION AND MODIFICATION

During the discussion, where the qualitative and quantitative aspects must be explored side by side for a full picture, new ideas will undoubtedly emerge which lead to the need for further estimates or modifications to existing estimates. Thus, for example, the helper and team may find that discussion around 'proportion of readers not renewing subscriptions' leads to the conclusion that a certain percentage of readers will always be lost, or that certain time lags are felt to be likely before any change in the journal will significantly affect its sales, or that the market includes a number of loyal readers below which circulation is unlikely to fall.

At the stage when the data requirements for constructing an initial Systems Dynamics model have been met the helper can then feed back the outcomes of some quantitative simulations alongside the qualitative map. To try and reduce the inevitable mystification surrounding the 'magic' numbers coming from the Systems Dynamics model he will need to try and ensure that the team members are aware of the assumptions underlying it and that they come from their own theories about their problem.

The feedback of the quantitative simulations may lead to further 'discoveries'. For example, it may be that the budget requirements for increasing the level of new introductions, according to the current arrangement, seem prohibitively high if any significant change in circulation is to be achieved; or that an increase in issue size above a certain level is punitive in terms of the current printing cost contract; or that the first proposals about changing the journal do not have the required effect on circulation. Certain figures may just seem 'stupid' or 'way out' and it is agreed that something must be wrong with some of the assumptions behind them. Some of these 'discoveries' will lead, for example, to a need to consider the political implications for effecting change in current policies within the organization, or to attend to the strong personal commitments of particular members of the team to a journal format which allows them to express their own interests but, by their own theories, does not coincide with the interests of potential readers. These are qualitative issues and, throughout, the quantitative and qualitative models will work side by side, as exploring the content and ramifications of one leads to a re-evaluation of the content and ramifications of the other.

The processes described in this chapter would continue until a problem definition has been negotiated which can, it is hoped, lead finally to the evolution of a portfolio of strategies that the journal team can be committed to. The concern is with finding methods of helping the clients reflectively and systematically make explicit, analyse and add to their own theories about their world so that they may devise ways of acting to meet their objectives. Within this context the role of quantitative modelling is no more, and *no less*, than a vehicle for capturing more fully, meaningfully and usefully the client's particular and personal images of his world than can be done by qualitative modelling alone.

Case Study

After the two meetings Jenny felt there were three immediate problems she had to tackle. The meeting with John, Justin and Alan had gone well and they had suggested the need for further work together without any prompting from her. However, this raised once again the question of Ian's involvement. Having started the process of getting the three managers talking to one another and sharing ideas in an apparently amicable and productive manner, Jenny felt reluctant to involve Ian before they had gone a bit further at least. Indeed she felt that if the process with the three of them continued to go well there was no reason why they could not present Ian with a fairly firm set of recommendations which they were all committed to.

However, she felt a need to 'suss out' Ian's attitude to a further continuation of the project beyond the original terms of reference and to his continued, at least for a while anyway, non-involvement. Also, of course, she needed to check this out with her own boss. Thirdly, Jenny felt that she had to do something fairly quickly about the possible disastrous outcomes of the meeting with Peter and Alan. If the two of them did not want to continue to work together, her own position would not be particularly pleasant. She would have failed in the one area in which Ian had hinted he was most interested, new-product development in the industrial products division. And this would obviously affect adversely the likelihood of Ian's agreeing to her continuing with Justin, John and Alan on consumer new-products development. Furthermore, her own boss was hardly likely to be pleased if she soured relationships with an important company division like Leakey.

With these thoughts running round her head and with them a need to go and see Alan and Peter as soon as possible so that she could at least try and redefine the situation in some more fruitful and promising way for them if necessary, it was only a couple of hours later that she popped her head round Alan's office door. She was particularly interested in Alan's reactions since he had been at the receiving end of Peter's attacks during the meeting. Alan smiled at her. "Well, that certainly gave me something to think about", he said. "Did you find it at all helpful?", asked Jenny, somewhat tentatively.

"Yes I did", replied Alan. "I have known Peter for a long time now, and I had no idea that he felt so strongly about the micro-chip arena. I am still not completely convinced that my own ideas about a better design for non-aqueous flows aren't right. In fact I'm convinced there's a market there but there's no reason in principle why that cannot go alongside a good look at computer-controlled valve systems. The latter is probably a long-term thing anyway, and would also almost certainly require a pretty major investment, not only in terms of plant and manpower — skills, I mean — but also marketing resources. I don't know how Ian would feel about that."

"How do you think he might feel", asked Jenny. "I really don't know", replied Alan. "His background is very much in consumer products. In fact I think it might be quite a good idea to get him involved in talking about it. After all, he is the man who has got to make the final decision about where we go, or certainly get any policy changes approved by the central board."

They talked for a while longer and Jenny left feeling a lot less anxious. She was not absolutely sure whether Alan had just been polite. His suggestion about Ian, for example, may have been a result of not wishing to repeat another acrimonious meeting with herself and Peter, which Ian's presence might avoid. But why not, she thought, and at least he had not suggested discontinuing the discussions. He had also agreed that Jenny could show Ian part of the qualitative model as a way of showing Ian the kind of work they had been doing, so long as it was a part which did not include any personal references to Ian. Now she had to go and find out how Peter felt. Peter was also in and once again the outcome was far better than she had expected. Peter was not as forthcoming as Alan, but Jenny had by now learned enough about Peter's interpersonal style not to be surprised or particularly concerned about this. Indeed he seemed more genuinely keen to continue than Alan had been, probably because he had done most of the talking at the meeting without any strongly negative comeback from Alan. He told her that he had thought the meeting had been worthwhile and added that "Alan was much more receptive than I had expected. Perhaps it's something to do with you being here and that technique you use. It's certainly very good at making you think through your ideas about something. It gives you something concrete to look at and talk to. So many meetings are spent with so much waffle that no one is really sure about what has been going on at the end."

"How would you feel if Ian became involved?", asked Jenny. Peter grimaced slightly. "The trouble is that he really doesn't know anything about the industrial area. I'm not sure that his presence would be at all helpful." He thought for a moment and then said, "Is that what you're suggesting? Well I suppose it would be one way of making sure that he did get to know more about it. I wonder though whether he will spend some time listening instead of wanting to put his oar in all the time. I suppose it could actually be quite useful if we could find a way of stopping him doing that."

Jenny spent some more time talking to Peter about the idea of Ian becoming involved, working on the idea that one way of getting Ian's support for any new product strategies in the industrial products area might well be getting him involved in their development, rather than offering him a *fait accompli*. Finally he agreed to Ian becoming involved with the proviso that "The three of us make sure that he does listen and doesn't try to run the show". He also agreed to let Jenny show part of his and Alan's cognitive map to Ian. Having got some dates from Peter for another meeting, her next step was to phone her boss, Arthur. She explained that it looked as if the project might be renegotiated for a longer time period and to include more than the original quantitative model, if Ian agreed. Arthur was pleased, and merely asked her to let him know the outcome of a discussion with Ian.

Finally, Jenny arranged to see Ian the next day. When she saw him, she explained to him that there had been a couple of highly productive meetings and that all those involved wanted to continue. At this point she showed him a 'group map' from the Peter—Alan meeting as his first introduction to cognitive mapping. He was not as interested as she had expected. "And how's Alan getting on with it?", he asked. "Is he beginning to think in wider terms?" Jenny replied that Alan had indeed said that he had found the activity useful. She certainly wasn't going to get into a discussion of whether Alan was or was not, or should be manipulated into, moving towards the directions Ian wanted. Ian seemed to realize that her reply had been deliberately evasive and that perhaps it had not been the most tactful question, and did not press further. "Good", he said.

Jenny decided that this was her opportunity to ask Ian if he would like to become involved in the next meeting with Peter and Alan. Ian looked surprised. "Yes, I suppose so", he said. "But I don't want to cramp their style. However, I suppose it would be helpful for me to know about the direction they are going in. What do Alan and Peter think about it?" "It was Alan who suggested it", said Jenny. "Well in that case, fine", replied Ian, adding, "So long as it doesn't take too much time."

Jenny then went on to suggest that it would be helpful if she could spend some more time with him on his own before any meeting, collecting his own ideas and then aggregating them with the existing Peter—Alan model. She felt a need to find out more about Ian's beliefs and interests before a threesome meeting which she would be less able to predict beforehand. He agreed and they then began to talk about the situation on the consumer product front. Here, of course, Jenny had to adopt a different tack and find some reason why Ian shouldn't be involved at this stage. She decided to use the excuse of Justin —

that Justin, as the junior member of the group and his assistant in Ian's previous job, might feel somewhat overwhelmed by Ian's presence and less able to contribute than if he weren't there. Ian accepted this argument and then went on explicitly to agree that Jenny should continue her involvement in Leakey with the new terms of reference.

He did ask, however, when she thought that both teams might have some final recommendations on new product development. He also asked where she was on the quantitative model that she had originally been commissioned to do. To the first question Jenny replied that it would be impossible at this early stage to be precise about the timing of the project, but after two further meetings with each team she would have a better idea. She suggested that this should be the next 'milestone' for reporting back and discussion with Ian, and he agreed to this. On the quantitative model she explained that she had just finished it within the original terms of reference. She would be happy to show it to him but she also felt that while it would undoubtedly provide some important input to the current work, this would probably result in the need to make some modifications to it. He might therefore prefer to wait till these had been done. Ian considered this and then said that he would still like to see it, perhaps at the next meeting they had arranged. Jenny went away well pleased with herself. "It's turning out all right", she grinned to herself.

Having dealt with her various causes of anxiety Jenny was now able to think about the next meeting with John, Justin and Alan. The Peter—Alan—Ian meeting would have to wait until after she had seen Ian on an individual basis anyway. John, Justin and Alan had all at various points in the meeting expressed a need to look at some of the financial implications of their ideas. Certainly Ian would expect any proposals from them to have the relevant numbers. However, the quantitative model she had already done did not incorporate the new ideas, particularly about new products, that had emerged in the last meeting. Nor did it incorporate the feedback loops that had been suggested. She decided that one way of proceeding would be to construct a crude Systems Dynamics model. This would take account of the feedback loops and could be used with the qualitative model for exploring the numerical implications of possible strategy options. Indeed it could be used with the existing quantitative model which would almost certainly provide data for the Systems Dynamics model and be modified as a result of work on the other two models.

Before, however, she converted the relevant parts of the cognitive map to an influence diagram she needed to put the new ideas that had come out of the meeting into the computer, 'regroup' and recheck for loops. Doing this she found that there were a couple of new sub-groups she wanted to establish as a way of structuring and managing the growing complexity of the group 'technological innovation'. This group had in the last meeting more clearly divided into two areas of interest, each of which could be expected to grow in content — "updating current products" and "move into new product areas such as plastics".

She was still working on the basis of there being one model covering both the industrial and consumer sections, since the ramifications of developments in both areas on one another would have to be looked at, at some time, by Ian and Alan at least and probably by the five managers together. However, at the moment the two areas were being looked at separately and since she had decided that she might have the computer models available to her clients at some stage, in addition to visual maps, she created two separate models for the two 'teams'.

Jenny looked at the feedback loops again, drawing them out in a visual map. This then became the basis for constructing the initial influence diagram for a Systems Dynamics model (see Figure 7.3). This in turn immediately led her to think about the kinds of questions she would want to explore with the managers at the next meeting, such as:

— the conventional, if nonetheless difficult, price—demand curve;
— the volume—cost relationship;
— the more intangible issues of the effect of varying product qualities on sales and greater concentration on brand or corporate image advertising,

and so on.

In preparing for the meeting Jenny followed a similar procedure to the last time. She produced a folder for each person, with the group titles and their relationships on the first page and then separate maps of the contents of groups

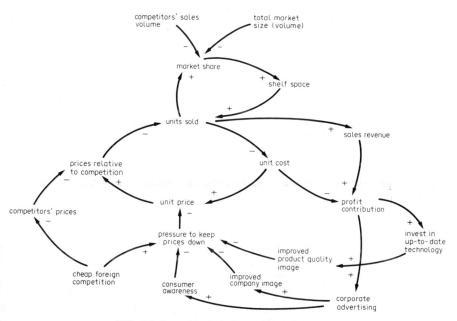

FIG. 7.3. Part of Jenny's first influence diagram.

on each page. The loop diagram also went on a separate page. She then reproduced the maps on larger flipchart sheets using the computer labels to speed up the process. She decided not to reproduce the influence diagram because it did not capture the same complexity of the managers' beliefs as a set of cognitive maps and might therefore be unhelpfully constraining. As the computer model had been previously, she saw the influence diagram primarily as an analyst's tool.

After the initial five-minute warm-up chat Jenny started the meeting by saying "At the last meeting you all suggested we should begin to look at some of the figures involved. Perhaps we could get into those by first having a look particularly at the loops diagram on page 2. Can I first check that it seems to you to accurately reflect what you all said last time?" John was the first one to respond. "Yes, I think it's fair. But it seems to me that it does miss one crucial bit of the price issue. We all know that most customers see some relationship between quality and price. At the moment it looks on the map as if the lower the price, the more we will sell. I don't think that's so. Apart from the obvious limit that cost has on how low you can go on price, I think that it could be positively disadvantageous to go too low, particularly if we think about this other idea down here – the idea of putting some money into improving our brand and company image. There's a limit, I think."

"Yes, I agree", said Justin. "Could you say what those limits are for your existing products?", asked Jenny after she had finished coding John's comments on the flipchart. Thus the discussion moved naturally into the pricing aspect of the model. John and Justin felt that they could categorize the existing products into various groups for the purpose of considering price–demand relationships and Alan agreed with these. Jenny asked each of them to write down separately their estimates of the effects of various price changes, within the range they felt to be acceptable, on volume sale, before putting them all up on the chart for discussion. As John, Justin and Alan talked about acceptable price ranges, the relationship between these and the company image, the likely response of customers to different prices, inevitably they also elaborated considerably their beliefs about the attitudes and preferences of their markets to Leakey products, and Jenny coded these.

They then went on to talk about the volume–cost relationships. At this point they referred to the marketing-plan documents they had all brought with them, and also asked Jenny to look at some of the figures from the quantitative work she had already done. By the end of a three-hour (and, Jenny felt, exhausting) meeting they had developed subjective estimates for all the relationships in and around the loops for existing products, working on indices from 1.0 (representing the current situation) for qualitative variables such as effect of image and quality changes. She had also agreed to do some further analysis of the price–demand curves before the next meeting.

The new-product area remained, however, relatively untouched, although they had made reference to it once or twice when talking about stronger branding of existing products and the way a move into plastics technology might affect such a process. It was at these points, however, that Alan showed most interest and particularly when the technical difficulties still associated with plastic plumbing ware were mentioned. "Perhaps Alan's interest in design improvement can be satisfied after all by something new", Jenny thought. She also felt that the discussion on new products would need to be more wide-ranging and unstructured initially than would be possible by working within the framework of a systems dynamics influence diagram. She also decided that the next meeting might be a good point at which to introduce her clients to the computer model. It might be interesting and useful for them if she were to input the ideas emerging from the meeting straight into the computer. They would then be able to explore the ramifications of these there and then in a way that would be increasingly difficult, as the model grew in size and complexity, to do quickly and easily through manual and visual manipulations. She also wondered whether if she fed back some simulations of a Systems Dynamics model concentrating on existing products at the beginning of the next meeting, they would become so absorbed in developing more qualitative ideas about existing products that they would not get on to new products that meeting at all.

As the meeting had progressed, she had found it more and more difficult to slow down the discussion by asking for quantity estimates. "Never mind the numbers, let's stay with the ideas", Peter had said after one of her questions about quantifying an estimate about the development of the non-aqueous market. The others seemed to agree, and so Jenny was persuaded that for the thinking they were doing at the present, she should stay with mapping. Problems seemed to be becoming clearer — and in some cases soluble — as they pieced together their ideas. "They may have to put numbers on some of these things later", Jenny had thought, "But at the moment Peter is right. Putting numbers down would just be a way of evading the question." She had made the decision to go on helping them build a joint map in that meeting, and to get round and have a chat individually with as many as possible of them before the next meeting, to discuss how much quantification could usefully be applied — or whether problems were being finished satisfactorily without that.

8
Closure

Each of the chapters of this book has been designed to introduce a different arena of thinking about the consulting/facilitating process. Early in the book we were mostly concerned with considering ways in which we see problems in organizations and how they come about. Here we were designing the 'spectacles' through which we see organizational decision-making. In our example Jenny was aware and thoughtful about the politics of her own situation with respect to her boss, her department and the client; she was interested in 'hidden agendas' and the fact that the problems belonged to people rather than the organization. Jenny recognized that the problem had been 'found' and that its history was relevant to her role; she explicitly negotiated a project which recognized that her role might change and that the nature of the problem would change. We continued by presenting a range of techniques which can help a consultant listen to the problem being presented by a client or actor in the situation. Some of these techniques were highly structured – repertory grids and the use of cards – whereas others were no more than suggestions about managing the very early stages of the consultant – client relationship. In our example we used the method of organizing cards to facilitate the client in his attempts to communicate about the problem as he saw it. Our concern was to encourage consultants to expend more than the usual amount of energy on helping the client to talk about his problem and, in most cases, more time listening to the client and crudely modelling his ideas. We stated clearly that we believe that problems are not usually presented in neat, tidy and concise ways but rather that they were messy, and rarely consisted primarily of crunchable numbers. We had already explained our view that the process of problem construction was usually undervalued and often regarded as a distraction from the rush to find solutions. As we arrived at the mid-point of the book we were still concerned as much with problem construction as solution, albeit a more definite modelling approach – the use of 'cognitive mapping'. We have tried to provide a lay guide to mapping as a method for modelling qualitative ideas and as a basis for facilitating the negotiation of a problem between members of a team, as well as a means for communicating about, negotiating over, and thinking through, the consequences of different solutions. And so, after we have presented two-thirds of the book we are still discussing problem construction . . .! "When are they going to concentrate on problem solution?", we could almost hear readers shouting.

HOLISTIC PROBLEM-SOLVING

In this, the last chapter, we are going to say more about it. We suspect that what we have to say is likely to be unsatisfactory for readers who believe in recommendations, final reports and such like as the end of problem-solving. For many consultants, and therefore, not surprisingly, many managers as well, their thoughts turn from the clarity of 'knowing what to do' to getting it done, or 'the problem of implementation'. Traditional demands, made through the literature and implicitly through the separation of solving from implementation, lead to a tendency to believe that time devoted to the activities of problem construction and making sense of the problem is time that is wasted. This tendency is often illustrated in teams by each member needing to express problems in terms of solution. That is, the culture of organizations requires their members to present their thinking about a problem by expressing possible solutions; otherwise their contributions are not seen as 'constructive'. The thinking that has gone into arriving at the suggested solution is camouflaged. The arena for problem-solving becomes a political fight between opposing solutions. The consequence of this approach is that little wisdom is shared, and positions rarely change because of learning about the nature of the problem from the intersubjectivity of team members; rather, positions change for reasons to do with short-term internal political games. If this is the case then it is unlikely that imaginative or creative strategies for action will surface.

Within this context of traditional approaches to working on problems we have, in this book, been trying to make the case that efficient team work is a consequence of facilitating thinking about problems rather than emphasizing so-called solution methods. We believe that the distinction between problem construction, making sense of problems, solving problems, and implementing solutions is less than clear. We ask you to consider carefully the process of discovering how to act in your own personal problem solving. The end of this process is mostly more akin to 'problem finishing' than it is to solution. Most people can recognize the experience of feeling a sense of 'closure', a point when it seems that there is an appropriate set of things to be done. What most of us do is to 'think around' a problem; we redefine it a few times, we mentally simulate some of the possible outcomes from possible courses of action, we try to make sense of the situation.[1] We don't do this in any particular order but rather cycle around — we think. When we get to that point at which we 'finish' thinking and want to act we know that we could have gone on thinking or might even have stopped thinking earlier. However, we usually expect to have arrived at a better set of actions than we would otherwise have done.

---

[1] See Eden (1981) for a discussion of the nature of the problem-solving process and its implications within an organizational setting. In addition this paper discusses some of the issues that arise from the bureaucratic needs within consulting practice.

A TAIL TO THE CONSULTANT'S TALE

Let us now consider Jenny and her activities. What was the solution? Was there an identifiable solution? Did the people involved in the project act differently as a consequence of her intervention? If so, how confident were any of them, including Jenny, that their actions would be 'better' than they would otherwise have been? Was the time and energy well used? In other words, to what extent did Jenny do a good job?

One way of considering Jenny's activities is to suppose that she had closed the project at the end of each of the stages reported at the end of each chapter. From the early meetings she had realized that the problem Ian wanted tackled had started life as a worry about how to bring Alan into line with his thinking on product development. Ian had devised a strategy for possibly relieving his worry by undertaking the legitimate exercise of "a review of product development using the sophisticated model building methods available at head office". Although Ian presented it as a forecasting exercise he reckoned he could get Jenny to bring Alan into it as 'link-man' and so by 'sleight of hand' get Alan to change his views so that they were 'more realistic'.

Let us consider the likely possibility that soon after the first couple of meetings with Jenny, Alan was beginning to see a wider view of product development — a view that seemed to Jenny to be close to the views held by Ian. This is likely because when somebody, such as Jenny, encourages a person to talk about some aspects of their job, and that person shows they have been listening, then they will usually find that the chance leads to an elaboration and modification of their own views. In the case we have considered Jenny used the cards and mapping as techniques for enabling Alan to be explicit and reflective about his views of his job and the future of the company. If it had been the case that Alan had moved, rightly or wrongly, to a view closer to that of Ian then she might have considered her job complete, to the extent that she judged Ian's root problem to have been 'solved'. Why should she, or should she not, close the project at this early stage? On the one hand, she has 'solved' the problem which Ian owned; but on the other she was not explicitly told about this version of the problem but rather was told to solve a legitimate problem. This double-bind is typical of those most of us face much of the time — if we close the project at this time then we shall not be faced with apathy from the client as we go on to 'solve' the publicly stated problem; however, if we try to publicly close the project then we are faced with somehow having to say to our client "you know that I know that the real problem is . . . but we can't talk about it" and our client having to excuse the fact that we have not done the job as it was publicly specified.[2]

Within all this description we are deliberately ignoring the political re-

---

[2] Eden and Sims (1979) discuss this bind and bluff in their paper 'On the nature of problems in consulting practice'.

percussions for us as helpers of explaining the rapidity of project completion to our own boss. We have also ignored the ethics of our professional role: for example, we may consider that it is our job to help the organization (whoever that may be), and within that we may regard the process of making Alan see things the same way as Ian sees them as wholly unacceptable to our role. In our case Jenny did not experience Alan changing to Ian's view. If she had carried on having 'solved' Ian's problem what are the possible reasons for her doing so? In Chapter 3 we discussed the process of finding problems in organizations, we noted that although problems change their form as they are made public these new problems are not necessarily of any less interest to the client. Thus Ian may have come to own a wider problem (an issue) which was certainly prompted by an unease about Alan but also began to include 'legitimate' problems about product mix, forecasts and their interplay with production, and their implication for product development. It is conceivable that he became interested in tapping the ideas of all his marketing managers and bringing them together into a coherent product-development policy.

Anyway, Jenny continued with her project, but we can see how the process of acting as careful 'listener' and modelling ideas and beliefs can enable a client to begin to see the problem differently to the extent that the problem 'dissolves'.[3] The same argument applies at any stage during the project, as it was executed by Jenny. She could easily have come to redefine and renegotiate her role, so that it was less that of problem-solver and more that of modeller/facilitator of a creative policy-evolution activity. However, she was to continue throughout the project with a view to acting as analyst/operational researcher/management scientist.

At the beginning of this chapter we said that we would consider the extent to which we had only discussed problem construction and left the reader with the nagging feeling that we had said nothing about problem-solving. We hope the above comments lucidly illustrate how difficult — and frequently unnecessary — it is to distinguish between construction and solution. Nevertheless we have not said much about those analytical skills and techniques which are more tradition-ally associated with the role of problem-solver.

We have not emphasized these aspects of Jenny's project or specifically presented the more established techniques of analysis simply because they are, for the most part, well established. But it might be helpful to elaborate about the role traditional techniques played in our case study. We usually find that the opportunity to use skills in mathematical, statistical, and computer techniques increases when extra time is devoted to problem construction of qualitative elements of an issue during the early stages of a project. For example, Jenny started with a fairly precise brief which would often lead directly to research in

---

[3] Ackoff and Emery (1972) define problem dissolution as 'the removal of a problem situation by [an individual] who is in it by a change in that individual's intentions'. They see this as distinct from 'solution' or 'resolution'.

amongst historical data, rebuilding cost data, and reading market research reports. This research would have led to 'wizardry back at the office' as the business of building a simulation model ensued. Instead Jenny devoted a great deal of time and energy to drawing together the main protagonists and working with them to develop and negotiate a qualitative model of the product development issue.

During the process of developing a view of the issue Jenny was able to gain the interest of Peter, Justin and John. In this way she had been able to build a view of product development from the experience, wisdom and judgement of those for whom the outcome of the project directly mattered. Each of the people involved had been able to gradually absorb the ideas of their colleagues and argue their points of view in a structured debate, where their views could easily be seen in the context of those of their colleagues. Jenny had given them a chance to work on the real problems of personal animosity, personal ambitions, and their own personal views of the future of the company. More significantly she had provided analysis of the maps by grouping ideas into a system of inter-connected problems that made up the complex issue they were addressing. It is at this stage that a successful and experienced analyst begins to spot the opportunities for prosecuting a variety of technical investigations. Jenny found that she got involved in a Network Analysis exercise to explore how long it would take to get new plant installed; she found herself working on a basic pricing model for the luxury fittings market; she was continually rebuilding her 'simple' simulation model so that all those involved could experiment with some of their ideas at a computer terminal during their meetings which were working on each of the cognitive maps that represented each problem in the issue; the analysis of the final cognitive map (which contained 367 concepts broken into 26 interconnected problems) she had located a sequence of feedback loops which were amenable to a crude Systems Dynamics model. The Systems Dynamics model was not constructed with the help of any special software (such as DYNAMO or DYSMAP) but was written in BASIC to work on a microcomputer. The model was based on the feedback loops that had been identified in the area of quality of the 'cheap' products, the investment in new plant, volume of sales, income available for investment, batch sizes, and reputation. During all of these studies she had been involved with Alan in digging out costing data, with Peter looking at a statistical method of analysing order sizes, and with some of the production staff who later got involved with the project in considering their production control methods (a peripheral project which blossomed into a distinct project for another member of the head office internal consulting team).

Given the above suggestion that analysis projects burgeon forth as a result of building a concern for constructing a picture of the problem which is the result of careful negotiation it is not surprising that some analysts use similar approaches in their search for work. For example, often an analyst will be in the company of managers for a variety of reasons (including lunching and socializing), during these occasions a manager will often absent-mindedly talk about something which is worrying him, the astute 'listening' analyst will mentally note a map which can then be put on paper later. Because maps are so transparent they can be the starting point for a further discussion with the manager about whether he (the analyst) had understood correctly, and as we have said before anyone usually feels flattered that someone has taken the trouble to hear his ideas. As the manager is eased into an interest in seeing his own views reflected back the analyst is able to introduce himself as having a potential role in working on certain aspects of the problem.

So, what actually did happen to Jenny? Over a total period of three months the group consisting of Alan, Peter, John and Justin was gradually expanded by the addition of Ian, the loss of Justin who was replaced by Bill, the replacement for Ian (Justin didn't get the job — possibly because of the way in which he behaved himself during this project), the addition of someone from the accounts department, and finally about half-way through the project by the addition of the production manager. Early events were designed by Jenny and she facilitated them using maps, statistical analyses displayed on flip-chart sheets, and using a computer terminal connected to the head office computer to run her simulation models and use COPE. At the end of three months they had jointly agreed a New Product Development Strategy which involved an expansion of Alan's group (mostly in reply to Alan's request for a microprocessor expert as well as a replacement for the man who had left). The Strategy required an extension to the factory, for which they would need both the approval of their board of directors and the planning director for the Group of companies. Towards the end of the project Ian pushed Jenny from her central role and controlled the meetings himself. Jenny thinks this point of changing control is connected with the point at which Ian was clear about what he wanted to happen and reckoned that he could guide the others accordingly. In her view this was linked to a significant shift in Ian towards a respect for Alan and possibly a realization that because Alan was not outwardly aggressive he had never given himself time to listen to what Alan had to say.

The General Scheme of Things

In this book we have tried to describe and demonstrate a range of approaches to the management of problem construction, problem definition, and working on 'soft' problems. At the end of this chapter we list a few of the case studies we have written about elsewhere so that a reader might gain a further insight into some of the work we have done using these approaches. It would be ludicrous for us to claim that the approaches we have described are complete or always appropriate. Many others are writing about approaches they have found helpful. For example, the Open University Systems group have been actively pursuing their own methods for managing 'soft' problems; Peter Checkland at the University of Lancaster has a well-developed approach to working with teams on 'messy' problems;[4] the work of Jim Radford in Canada is well established as a method for considering conflict and significant actors in policy problems,[5] and the related (but more theoretical) work by Peter Bennett on 'hypergames' is showing promise.[6] Ken Bowen has followed his work at the Defence Operational Analysis Establishment with current work on problem construction — we hope he will be writing about this work in the near future.

[4] See Checkland (1981).
[5] See, for example, Radford (1977).
[6] For a recent example of their intentions for the use of hypergame analysis in practice see Bennett, Huxham and Dando (1981).

CASE STUDIES

Eden, C. and Smithin, T. (1979) Operational Gaming in Action Research. *European Journal of Operational Research, 3*, 450–458.

Eden, C., Jones, S., Sims, D. and Gunton, H. (1979) Images into Models. *Futures*, February.

Eden, C. and Jones, S. (1980) Publish or Perish? A case study. *Journal of the Operational Research Society, 31*, 131–139.

Eden, C. and Jones, S. (1980) Comment on 'Publish or Perish'. *Journal of the Operational Research Society, 31*, 1109–1111.

Armstrong, T. and Eden, C. (1977) *Making Sense of Purpose.* Centre for the Study of Organizational Change and Development: University of Bath.

Jones, S. and Eden, C. (1981) OR in the Community. *Journal of the Operational Research Society, 32*, 335–345.

Sims, D. and Eden, C. (1983) Involving Managers in the Future. *Journal of the Long Range Planning Society*, June.

Armstrong, T. and Eden, C. (1979) An Exploration of Occupational Role: an exercise in team development. *Personnel Review, 8*, 20–23.

Eden, C. and Sims, D. (1981) Computerized Vicarious Experience: the future for management induction? *Personnel Review.*

Sims, D. and Jones, S. (1981) Explicit problem modelling: an intervention strategy. *Group and Organisation Studies, 6*, 486–498.

Smithin, T. and Sims, D. (1983) Helping Charity Officers Reflect on Their Work. *Voluntary Action*, forthcoming.

References

Ackoff, R. L. (1974) *Redesigning the Future*. New York: Wiley.

Ackoff, R. L. (1979) 'The future of operational research is past.' *Journal of the Operational Research Society*, 30, 93–104.

Ackoff, R. L. and Emery, R. E. (1972) *On Purposeful Systems*. London: Tavistock.

Allison, G. T. (1971) *Essence of Decision: Explaining the Cuban Missile Crisis*. Waltham: Little, Brown.

Alonzo, W. (1968) 'Predicting best with imperfect data.' *American Institute of Planners Journal*, July pp. 248–255.

Armstrong, T. and Eden, C. (1979) 'An exploration of occupational role – an exercise in team development.' *Personnel Review*, Winter.

Axelrod, R. (ed.) (1976) *Structure of Decision*. Princeton, N.J.: University of Princeton Press.

Bachrach, P. and Baratz, M. S. (1970) *Power and Poverty: Theory and Practice*. New York: Oxford University Press.

Bannister, D. and Fransella, F. (1971) *Inquiring Man*. Harmondsworth: Penguin.

Bennett, P. G., Huxham, C. S. and Dando, M. R. (1981) 'Shipping in crisis: a trial run for "live" application of the hypergame approach.' *Omega* (forthcoming).

Bennis, W. G. (1969) *Organization Development: Its Nature, Origins and Prospects*. Reading, Mass.: Addison-Wesley.

Berger, P. L. and Luckmann, T. (1966) *The Social Construction of Reality*. New York: Doubleday.

Burns, T. (1969) 'On the plurality of social systems', in T. Burns (ed.) *Industrial Man*. Harmondsworth: Penguin.

Checkland, P. (1981) *Systems Thinking, Systems Practice*. London: Wiley.

Cook, S. L. (1976) Putting operational research to work in the organization. Unpublished lecture notes. Birmingham: University of Aston.

Coyle, R. G. (1977) *Management System Dynamics*. London: Wiley.

Easterby-Smith, M. (1980) 'How to use repertory grids in HRD.' *Human Resource Development*, 4, 2.

Eden, C. (1974) 'On the role of a decision analyst.' University of Bath: School of Management.

Eden, C. (1978) 'Operational research and organizational development.' *Human Relations*, 31 (8) 657–674.

Eden, C. (1981) 'The influence of OR on decision making in organisations,' presented as a keynote address to the Australian Society for Operational Research, Sydney, August.

Eden, C., Jones, S. and Sims, D. (1979) *Thinking in Organizations*. London: Macmillan.

Eden, C., Jones, S., Sims, D. and Smithin, T. (1981) 'Intersubjective issues and issues of intersubjectivity.' *Journal of Management Studies*, 18 (1) 37–47.

Eden, C. and Sims, D. (1977) 'Problem definition between consultant and client.' University of Bath: Centre for the Study of Organizational Change and Development.

Eden, C. and Sims, D. (1979) 'On the nature of problems in consulting practice.' *Omega*, 7 (2) 119–127.

Eden, C. and Wheaton, G. (1980) 'In favour of structure. . . .' University of Bath: Centre for the Study of Organizational Change and Development.

Egan, G. (1975) *The Skilled Helper*. Monterey, California: Brooks/Cole Publishing.

Forrester, J. W. (1961) *Industrial Dynamics*. Boston: MIT Press.

112   *Messing About in Problems*

Forrester, J. W. (1971) *World Dynamics.* Cambridge, Mass.: Wright-Allen.

Galbraith, J. K. (1974) *The New Industrial State* (2nd ed.). Harmondsworth: Penguin.

Harary, F., Norman, R. and Cartwright, D. (1965) *Structural Models: An Introduction to the Theory of Directed Graphs.* New York: Wiley.

Jones, R. and Lakin, C. (1978) *The Carpet Makers.* Maidenhead: McGraw-Hill.

Jones, S. and Eden, C. (1980) 'O.R. in the community.' *J. Opl. Res. Soc.*, 32, 335–345.

Kelly, G. A. (1955) *The Psychology of Personal Constructs.* New York: Norton.

Kelly, G. A. (1972) *A Theory of Personality.* New York: Norton.

Kepner, C. H. and Tregoe, B. B. (1965) *The Rational Manager.* New York: McGraw-Hill.

Lukes, S. (1974) *Power: a Radical View.* London: Macmillan.

McLean, A., Sims, D., Mangham, I. and Tuffield, D. (1982) *Organization Development in Practice.* London: Wiley (in preparation).

Mangham, I. L. (1977) 'Definitions, interactions and disengagement.' *Small Group Behaviour*, 8 (4) 487–510.

Mangham, I. L. (1979) *The Politics of Organizational Change.* London: Associated Business Press.

Meadows, D. H., Meadows, D. L., Randers, J. and Behrens, W. W. (1972) *The Limits to Growth.* London: Earth Island.

Neisser, U. (1976) *Cognition and Reality.* San Francisco: Freeman.

Perrow, C. (1972) *Complex Organizations.* Glenview, Ill.: Scott Foresman.

Pettigrew, A. (1973) *The Politics of Organizational Decision Making.* London: Tavistock.

Pettigrew, A. (1977) 'Strategy formulation as a political process.' *International Studies of Management and Organization*, 7 (2) 78–87.

Radford, K. J. (1977) *Complex Decision Problems.* Reston, VA: Reston Publishing Co.

Roberts, F. S. (1976) 'Strategy for the Energy Crisis,' in Axelrod, R., *Structure of Decision.* Princeton: Princeton University Press.

Rokeach, M. (1973) *The Nature of Human Values.* New York: Free Press.

Silverman, D. (1970) *The Theory of Organizations.* London: Heinemann.

Sims, D. (1978) *Problem Construction in Teams.* Ph.D. Thesis, University of Bath.

Sims, D. (1979) 'A framework for understanding the definition and formulation of problems in teams.' *Human Relations*, 32 (11) 909–921.

Slee Smith, P. I. (1971) *Think Tanks and Problem Solving.* London: Business Books.

Stearns, N. S., Bergan, T. A., Roberts, E. B. and Cavazos, L. F. (1978) 'A System Intervention for Improving Medical-School–Hospital Interrelationships.' *Journal of Medical Education*, 53, 464–472.

Thomas, W. I. and Thomas, D. S. (1928) *The Child in America: Behavior Problems and Progress.* New York: Knopf.

Wittgenstein, L. (1953) *Philosophical Investigations.* Oxford: Oxford University Press.

Young, K. (1977) 'Values in the policy process.' *Policy and Politics*, 5, 1–22.

Appendix
Computer Assistance

To use the techniques we have described in this book, the problem-helper needs no more aids than paper and pen. Nor need helpful models be large models. We do, however, believe that modern tools like the computer may be useful if they are available, and clearly a computer could fruitfully be employed to assist in the analysis of a large body of complex data. To this end we have developed a suite of computer programs called COPE (Cognitive Policy Evaluation) specifically to assist with the handling of cognitive maps. This appendix describes the most important features of the COPE software and its use. We give some description of the nature of the software, and then go on to talk about how data can be entered into COPE models, and how the contents of the models may be viewed. Next, we consider how a model may be explored by a helper or his client, and then we describe some of the forms of exploration which might be undertaken by a helper but which would probably not be used interactively by a client. Finally, we illustrate the sort of output that can be obtained by using COPE, taking the cognitive map in Chapter 7 (Figure 7.1) as an example. The software is currently available in two versions, one for mini and mainframe computers, and one for microcomputers operating under CP/M. For simplicity we shall restrict ourselves here to describing the microcomputer version.

USING THE SOFTWARE

The software has developed gradually through our work with clients. Using it with clients as it was developed has helped us to concentrate on the need to make the interactions with the computer friendly and relevant. The chosen method for operating COPE is command orientated, whereby the user enters one of a number of directives at the main prompt (COPE>). This was found in practice to be a more helpful approach than the alternative method of imposing a set order or sequence to events by guiding the user via a series of questions.

There is also a comprehensive hierarchy of HELP messages which itemizes the commands available to the user within COPE. The command structure is composed of a series of mostly single character operatives, which are easily memorable, and can be built up in a combination to form a more complex demand. Thus COPE can be operated at a simple level very easily, but can also become a very powerful tool for analysis by the problem-helper who takes advantage of its full capabilities.

ENTERING DATA

Entering data is quite simple. A concept is identified by a concept number and following text. Concept poles are separated by slashes, with a void pole shown by two consecutive slashes:

COPE>1=/production output dropping quickly/steady production output/
COPE>2=/more/less/investment
COPE>3=/high wastage//

Monotonic concepts are entered without slashes:

COPE>4=level of advertising revenue.

Relationships are entered at the COPE prompt as follows:

COPE>1+3-2.4 shows a positive causal relationship from 1 to 3, a negative causal relationship from 1 to 2, and a connotative link between 1 and 4. Any of the constituent parts of this description can be overwritten by retyping them. If the user wants to delete the concept, he simply types D followed by the code (e.g. COPE>D18 will delete concept 18 and all its relationships). Data may be entered or changed at any point.

GROUPS

In Chapter 4 we discussed how the content of a model may be structured into clusters of related concepts or different areas of concern within an issue. Data can thus be held at the level of a group, and the group structure is hierarchical; that is, a group can contain sub-groups as well as a number of concepts. Grouping can be done automatically or manually or both. Autogrouping follows the procedure discussed in Chapter 4, whereby crucial concepts which appear to define a particular area of concern are identified. For example, typing the command COPE>G5$10 creates a group 5 based upon the key concept 10. With a number of groups identified in this way, the AUTO command then automatically traces back and includes in each group all those concepts which have consequences for the key concept naming the group, until another key 'group' concept is reached, and another group commences.

Manual grouping involves labelling a group (e.g. COPE>G1=working as a team) and then listing the concepts and other groups contained within it, e.g. COPE>G1;20;21;30;G2;100. Additional concepts can also be added to 'automatic' groups in this way. The use of grouping is one way in which a client can conveniently assess concepts.

EXPLORING A MODEL

Often after some initial interviews, we enter a model and then invite a client to explore its content and ramifications at the computer. There are a number of options to enable a person to view the contents of a model. The first of these are the LIST commands (COPE>L), which enable a person to view selected parts of the model before proceeding to explore the concepts of interest to him. Typically, a client may begin his exploration by listing the groups and then looking at the contents of a particular group in more detail. The command COPE>LG lists the group titles, and then, for example, COPE>LGC1 will list all the concepts in group 1. COPE>LGH will show any hierarchical relationships between groups. COPE>L lists all concepts while COPE>LR lists all their relationships. COPE> L1,10 lists concepts 1 to 10.

Another way of finding items of particular interest is to search for key phrases or words with the COPE>L 'anyphrase' command. For example, a housing officer might want to look for all concepts containing the phrase 'housing association' if this is the topic of interest at the time. A person may also wish to identify, evaluate or elaborate upon those concepts at the head of chains of beliefs which represent the believed outcomes of sequences of events, like concept D in Figure A.1. The command COPE>LH will list all such 'head' concepts in a model.

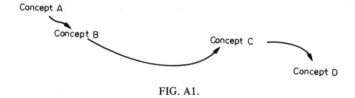

FIG. A1.

In a similar way, the command COPE>LT lists all those concepts at the end or 'tail' of a chain of beliefs, like concept A in Figure A.1., which a helper might request a client to further elaborate or explain. A further way of pinpointing significant concepts is to identify those which have a relatively high number of links to them in the form of explanations, consequences or connotative links, as one crude measure of their relative centrality. COPE>LCC will print out the number of causal links leading directly into or out of any concept and the number of connotative relationships. This may also help in the identification of crucial concepts for grouping.

COMMANDS TO EXPLORE THE CONTENTS

Once a person has used these options to identify concepts of interest to him, he can then explore them in the following ways:

(i) Consequences

If he types C followed by the concept code (e.g. COPE>C25) the computer will search for and print out each chain of beliefs leading from the concept. Where a chain branches into two or more further consequences it will stop, and indicate by dots attached to the consequence at this point that there are further consequences which can be explored. More specifically, the computer will search in terms of which ever pole of the construct is specified. The first pole is specified by default.

(ii) Explanations

The letter E followed by a concept code (e.g. COPE>E34) will obtain the explanations of the concept in a similar way.

(iii) Connotative links

The K command will display all concepts that are connotatively linked to the specified concept (e.g. COPE>K24). The computer will also print a (K) after a concept if there are any connotative links to that concept.

(iv) General explorations

The letter X followed by a concept code will obtain the consequences of that concept, in the same way as C would, the explanations of it, in the same way as E, and any connotative links, in the same way as K.

(v) Routes

If the client wishes to explore the links between two specified concepts, the computer will execute a path analysis, looking for and printing out any routes between them (e.g. COPE>C10,5 will search for any routes from concept 10 to 5; COPE>E2,12 will search for any explanations for concept 2 from concept 12).

OUTPUT FROM THE MODEL

For the kind of model that we are talking about in this book, it is vital to produce output in a form which makes sense to the client, and is seen by him as applicable to his special needs. We have therefore paid considerable attention to providing more understandable and flexible output than is usual from computer models. This includes:

(i) Options to abbreviate or suppress tedious or repetitious sections of text.
(ii) Options to print self-adhesive labels of any concept which could, for example, be used as the basis of a wall chart or other form of large visual display.
(iii) Options to produce a small section (about 30 concepts) of the map on a

computer graphics screen, or Diablo printer. The first of these also enables an interactive use of the map using a light pen.

(iv) Option to store any part of the output in a file, and also to retain all commands entered.

These options and printing commands have been designed to be easily usable and memorable by the client. For example, placing MAP before any command will produce a two-dimensional map rather than the usual linear text output for that command.

THE HELPER'S USE OF COPE

The extent to which the helper becomes involved in entering data and helping the client to explore the map varies from project to project, depending partly on personal preference, and also upon the negotiated aims of the work. As the above brief description shows, it is quite easy for a client to enter data and to explore the model without the helper's aid. An advantage of COPE, however, is that there are analytic aids available if needed, of which we shall enumerate four here.

(i) Merging models and concepts

The helper can combine two models if he wishes. He must ensure that the concept codes in each model do not coincide, and a renumbering command is available for doing this. Thus, for example, while in Model A he can add Model B by the command COPE>ADD B. This may be useful in a group situation where the helper wishes to combine a number of individual models to produce an aggregate model. The helper can also merge concepts and groups. If, for example, in an aggregate model concepts 18 and 30 are sufficiently similar that they can be merged (see Chapter 6), COPE>18=30 removes concept 30 and incorporates all its relationships with those of concept 18. Groups can be merged in exactly the same way; e.g. COPE>MG1=G20 will remove group 20 and add its concepts to those in group 1.

Merging thus creates, especially in a group situation, some links and connections between separate models. Thus, for example, an individual can see how a policy he has suggested within his own view of a situation may have different ramifications in terms of other views of the situation.

(ii) Autogrouping

As we have said, this facility enables a helper to create a group automatically from the identification of crucial concepts.

(iii) Grouping with the subsystem

A subsystem is a part of the model which can be built up in a number of ways. If the helper types SUB before a List or explore command, the concepts referred to in that command will be placed in a subsystem. Thus, for example, COPE>SUB1 L 'housing' will add all concepts containing the word 'housing' into subsystem 1 (there are 4 subsystems available). COPE>G1;SUB1 would then place the contents of subsystem 1 in group 1. There is also a facility to transfer the contents of the subsystem to a separate model or file; e.g. COPE> SAV SUB1, HOUSING will store the contents of subsystem 1 in a separate COPE model called HOUSING.

(iv) Loops

As discussed in Chapter 4, the existence of feedback loops within the causal chains of beliefs can be a significant aspect of the data for a client. COPE>LOOP will search for any loops, and print out the concepts in the loops with the signs of the relationships in the loop, so that they can be examined more systematically if required.

COPE – BRIEF GUIDE TO COMMANDS

Full details on any COPE command are available, when using COPE, by typing HELP and the command you wish to look at. For example, HELP C, HELP AUTO.

ADD   – add contents of one model to another
AUTO – create groups by the automatic grouping procedure
BYE   – exit from a COPE session
C   – explore the consequences of a concept
D   – delete concepts, links, groups and title lines
DEL   – delete COPE files
DIR   – listing of all COPE files, including archived files
E   – explore the explanations of a concept
G   – create group names, and add concepts to groups manually
GET   – get a model and append contents of current model to it
HELP   – view HELP messages
K   – list any connotative links to a concept
L   – list portions of a COPE model
L"   – list any concepts containing the specified string, e.g. 'decisions'
L#   – list the protected concepts
LCC   – list total of all concepts immediately linked to given concept
LG   – list group names
LGC   – list group contents
LGH   – list group hierarchies (groups which contain other groups)
LGR   – list group relationships (which groups particular concepts are in)
LH   – list Head concepts (concepts with no consequences)
LI   – list all concepts leading directly into a concept
LT   – list Tail concepts (concepts with no explanations)

LAB   — output in form of 10 X 8 mm labels
LOOP   — search for all feedback loops
M   — merge concepts or groups
MAC   — create a macro file of COPE commands
MAP   — output in form of a map (graphics, diablo or at user terminal)
MAT   — output in form of a matrix
NUM   — automatically number concepts on entry
P   — direct output from any command to another terminal
REN   — renumber concepts in a COPE file
RENG   — renumber groups in a COPE file
SAV   — create a copy of a COPE file, or part of a COPE file
SIZE   — gives the current size and allowed maximums of a COPE file
SQU   — tidy up COPE file
SUBn   — use a temporary storage region (subsystem)
T   — print or insert a title for a COPE file
TB   — trace from a concept to all Heads and from all Tails
TH   — trace from a concept to all Heads
TT   — trace from all Tails to a concept
USE   — bring a COPE file into use
X   — explore both consequences and explanations for a concept
/A   — change linking text to arrows
/D   — make diablo printer available for maps
/F   — change text to continuous prose without concept numbers
/G   — make the graphics terminal available for maps
/LAB   — change the specified terminal at which labels will be printed
/O   — limit output on VDU to 10 lines at a time
/P   — change the terminal to which the P command directs output
/T   — suppress the repetition of concept description during explore commands
@   — run a COPE macro file, or log file

ARCHIVE — to archive COPE files, and save disc space
RECALL — to recall archived files so that they can be used

>COPE   SUPER COPE   02-DEC-80

COPE>USE MAGAZINE
MAGAZINE MODEL   *— Model title*

COPE>LG
G1   Attractiveness to readers $6
G2   Editorial quality $24
G3   Unattractive to advertisers $2
G4   Not working as a team $18
G5   No commitment of sales reps $11

G6   Readiness of senior management to invest
     money $14

COPE>LGH   *– List Group Hierarchy*

G1   ; G2

G1   ; G6

G4   ; G1

G1   ; G3

G1   ; G4

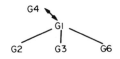

COPE>LGC2

G2   Editorial quality $24   *– List contents of group 2*

GROUPS: *– (no subordinate groups*
                                     in this case)

CONCEPTS:

  6   Attractiveness to readers

19   /Low/Higher/staff morale

20   /Fixed/Variable/ad–ed ratio

21   /Working blindfold/Can plan in advance/

22   Editorial staff problems

23   /Safe middle of the road/Adventurous and
        controversial/editorial

24   Editorial quality

25   /Covering very best in the field//

26   /Aim at lower end of market//

27   /Glossy magazine format//

28   /Where most of our readers are//

29   /Not enough/More active/contact with trade

30   /Current/Better/printer's timing

35   /Old news/First with the news/

COPE>X24   *– explore the explanations*

24   An increase in Editorial quality   *and consequences for the*
        can be explained by   *positive pole of concept*

–35 ..First with the news   *24*
        and/or can be explained by

25   Covering very best in the field
        which can be explained by

27   Glossy magazine format . . .

24   An increase in Editorial quality
        can be explained by

26 ..Aim at lower end of market
        and/or can be explained by

–23   Adventurous and controversial editorial
        and/or can be explained by

-22 ..a decrease in Editorial staff problems
24 An increase in Editorial quality
    can lead to
6 ..an increase in Attractiveness to readers . . .

COPE>E-22
-22 A decrease in Editorial staff problems
    can be explained by
-21 Can plan in advance
    which can be explained by
-20 Variable ad–ed ratio . . .
-22 A decrease in Editorial staff problems
    can be explained by
-19 Higher staff morale . . .
    which can be explained by
-1 ..Increasing circulation . . .

– list explanations for the negative pole of concept 22

COPE>L 'staff'
19 /Low/Higher/staff morale
22 Editorial staff problems
COPE>LOOP

– list the concepts containing the word 'staff'
– check for feedback loops

LOOP 1   LENGTH 6   POSITIVE
+1 /Declining/Increasing/circulation
+2 /Unattractive/Attractive/to advertisers
-3 Number of advertising pages sold
-5 Issue size
-6 Attractiveness to readers
+7 People not renewing subscriptions
+1 /Declining/Increasing/circulation

	1	2	3	5	6	7
1	0	1	0	0	0	0
2	0	0	-1	0	0	0
3	0	0	0	1	0	0
5	0	0	0	0	1	0
6	0	0	0	0	0	-1
7	1	0	0	0	0	0

– matrix for loop 1 is given

LOOP 2   LENGTH 2   POSITIVE

+4 number of editorial pages
+L1 POSITIVE LOOP 1 LENGTH 6
+4 number of editorial pages
    4 L1

```
 4   0   1
L1   1   0
```

LOOP 3   LENGTH 2   POSITIVE

```
+8   New sales
+L2  POSITIVE LOOP   2 LENGTH   2
+8   New sales

     8   L2

 8   0   1
L2   1   0
```

Index